IMPACT OF ENGLISH AND MAJOR INDIAN LANGUAGES ON THE TRIBAL LANGUAGES OF WESTERN ODISHA

IMPACT OF ENGLISH AND MAJOR INDIAN LANGUAGES ON THE TRIBAL LANGUAGES OF WESTERN ODISHA

Seemita Mohanty

GYAN

The Publication of this book was financially supported by ICSSR and the responsibility for the facts stated, opinions expressed or conclusions reached are entirely that of the author and ICSSR accepts no responsibility for them.

ICSSR Consultant

Dr. Vivek Kumar, Centre for Social Science Studies, School of Social Sciences, JNU, New Delhi-110067.

ISBN : 978-81-212-1233-3

Price: ₹

First Published 2014

Published by

Gyan Publishing House
23, Main Ansari Road, Daryaganj,
New Delhi - 110002
Phones : 23282060, 23261060
Fax : (011) 23285914
E-mail: books@gyanbooks.com
website: gyanbooks.com

Laser Typesetting: Rajender Vashist, Delhi
Printed at: G. Print Process, Delhi

Cataloging in Publication Data--DK
Courtesy: D.K. Agencies (P) Ltd. <docinfo@dkagencies.com>

Mohanty, Seemita.
Impact of English and major Indian languages on the tribal languages of western Odisha / Seemita Mohanty.
p. cm.
Includes bibliographical references (p.) and index.
ISBN 9788121212333

1. English language--India--Sundargarh (District)--Influence on Adivasi Odia language. 2. Adivasi Odia language--India--Sundargarh (District)--Foreign elements--English. 3. India--Languages--Influence on Adivasi Odia language. 4. Tribes--India--Sundargarh (District)--Languages. I. Title.

DDC 420 23

Contents

Foreword

Nothing gives more pleasure to the head of an institution of higher learning than a major scholastic work coming out of the pen of a faculty colleague. The pleasure is doubled when the subject of the work is socially relevant and the book ends with a set of concrete, implementable recommendations. It is a unique pleasure for me to write the following paragraphs introducing the book on the influence of English and main-stream Indian languages on the numerous tribal languages and dialects of Western Odisha by my colleague Prof. Seemita Mohanty.

Nearly four decades ago, when I was a young post-doc at a US laboratory, during a lunch break under the blue California sky, I was called by a group of Chinese friends sitting on the next table. They asked me a question: "What is the equivalent word of "Privacy" in Hindi?" I searched my memory hard, but found no word in Hindi, Odia, Bengali or Sanskrit that would describe the common English word which most Americans hold close to their hearts. Our culture does not honour privacy, and hence our forefathers felt no necessity of inventing a word for it. My friends told me, there is no equivalence of privacy in Mandarin or Cantonese. A language is not only a means of communication between individuals, but also a vehicle for transmitting emotion, culture and higher values of life. Some years later, I asked friends: what is the English word for "Abhiman"; I am still waiting for a satisfactory answer.

A friend of mine living in Canada once told me, the Eskimo language has twenty words for the solid form of water; English probably has five and my mother tongue has just one. For the Eskimo, a quick and accurate description of the type of snow or ice that he is expected to meet on a hunting trip can mean the difference between life and death. The hunter in Andamans has no reason to clutter up his brain with such cold objects. Words originate to express physical and emotional needs; sentences and phrases add artistic compositions to reflect happenings in the higher levels of the human brain that take centuries to evolve and mature.

The tribal societies of India, living in harmony with nature, mountains, rivers and forests evolved their own vocabulary, rich in words and phrases synchronised with their unique surroundings. Unfortunately they have little to offer to effectively articulate the needs and thoughts of the factory worker, government servant and the international traveler. It is inevitable that in the war of languages, the weaker species would fade away with time. What is desirable, however, is that the unique and potentially advantageous components of the vanquished languages enrich the victors, thus saving till eternity the contributions of hundred generations of creative men and women. Unfortunately the juggernaut of socio-economic change is moving fast leaving no scope for upstream flow of linguistic resources.

Prof. Mohanty, through her elegant literary style and painstaking research has quantitatively expressed this sorry state of affairs; but she has gone a step farther; she has conceived and articulated a set of mitigation measures that, if implemented, can slow down, though not eliminate the process of social change. Then, I believe, the surviving languages, tribal or mainstream, will get the time to absorb the best features of their dying cousins.

What Prof. Mohanty has observed, and so nicely articulated, for tribal languages is also true to a large extent for major Indian languages facing the onslaught of English.

Many more children today are learning their first school lessons in English than they ever did during the British rule. Sanskrit, the Indian language with well-articulated structural features for describing scientific and technical thoughts, is far more deeply forgotten today than it ever did under the British. Early education in a foreign tongue, particularly among the more gifted children with higher access to superior schooling facilities, is giving birth to a unique phenomenon: complete disconnect between education and profession. The Indian professional, be it in industry or in agriculture, in international trade or day to day life, thinks in two different planes – one for writing exams and making speeches, and another for getting things done for oneself, one's family and one's employer. Innovation is the obvious victim.

Prof. Mohanty, in this beautiful book, has thrown light on one large aspect of a much larger linguistic – demographic – social issue. I am sure this book will be liked by readers from all walks of life, from plain office babus to the most serious researchers. On behalf of NIT Rourkela, the unique institute where every faculty, staff and student strives to attain his or her potential, I introduce this beautiful work of my able colleague to the readers across the world.

Prof. Sunil Kr. Sarangi, FNAE
Director
National Institute of Technology
Rourkela (Odisha)

Preface

This book is the outcome of a study that was undertaken with financial assistance from Indian Council of Social Science Research (ICSSR), New Delhi, to assess the impact of English and major Indian languages on the tribal languages of western Odisha. Odisha is a tribal dominated state witl as many as 62 tribal communities being natives to the state. Census 2001 reports that these 62 tribes of Odisha speak as many as 74 dialects. Isn't it an irony, therefore, that sitting in the midst of such linguistic diversity, what we actually encounter today is sad state-of-affairs, where language maintenance among tribals is almost non-existent. Sundargarh, the study area of this particular project, is a tribal dominated district of the state of Odisha. The district is home to quite a few indigenous tribal groups who hugely enrich the cultural milieu of the place. Throughout the year, during some specific festivities, be it the morning hours or evening hours, it is not unusual to come across tribal men and women, young and old, singing and dancing to the tunes of tribal songs and music, even in the middle of a busy market place or in open spaces, specifically designated for such functions. To an outsider, or a tourist, it appears to be something new and unique and a real pleasure to watch. The tourist goes back feeling happy and satisfied with the obvious richness and diversity of our cultural heritage. But the reality is very far from what is being perceived in general.

Language has always been extensively accepted as a major indicator of one's cultural identity. But today the tribals no longer perceive their native languages as economically viable. As a result, the languages are losing fast their social viability. My job at a place like Rourkela, which is strategically located right in the middle of a tribal belt, has been instrumental in bringing me face to face with this bleak language condition, which subsequently encouraged me to take up such a study. In the context of such language endangerment situation, this book is a sincere attempt to highlight the plight of our tribal languages which are today on the verge of becoming dead languages. More importantly, the book also urges its readers to generate understanding and sensitivity to the needs of our tribal languages, thereby, educational policies appropriate to the tribal context could be designed, and that could pave the path for long-term development of the languages which is the need of the hour. Working towards growth, development and modernisation of tribal areas without well-defined educational policies could sometimes be counter-productive. Language is integral to the existence and development of any culture and it has to be nurtured and nourished accordingly if we want our cultural diversity to be sustained and be a part of the nation's overall progress.

I wish to conclude with sincere acknowledgement of the financial assistance received from the Indian Council of Social Science Research, New Delhi, without which the timely production of the current publication would not have been possible. I also gratefully acknowledge the tremendous amount of information that I have received from all the primary and secondary sources that I have referred to in my work, which have been invaluable for a study like this. A profound sense of indebtedness and gratitude is reserved for my esteemed Director, Prof. Sunil Kumar Sarangi, for being a constant source of inspiration and motivation, and for taking time out from his busy schedule to write the foreword for the book. My thanks and appreciation also goes to my colleagues in the Department of Humanities and Social Sciences at NIT, Rourkela, and other local people who have willingly and happily helped me out to the best of their abilities. I am thankful to my two Research Assistants, Manasi Rani Gahana and Parameswara Mahanta, for their assistance in data collection and data entry. My final gratitude is towards my parents; to my father, who is no more with us, but without whose unfaltering support and concern, I would not have been able to complete the study, and to my mother, for being there whenever I needed her. Heartfelt thanks are also reserved for my brother Sambit, for readily giving me the photograph of the two beautiful tribal girls, for the cover design, from his personal collection. Last but not least, I am thankful to the Production team at Gyan Publishing House for their meticulous editing and for the quick publishing process.

Seemita Mohanty

List of Tables, Figures and Illustrations

Figures

Illustrations

1
Introduction

Background of the Study

According to the Census 2001, the tribal people of India account for about 8.2 per cent of India's total population. They number about 85 million as per the Census 2001. They are mostly concentrated in 10 states of the Central Highlands, the Chhottanagpur plateau, the Eastern Ghats in Odisha and Andhra Pradesh and the western parts of the country. These regions account for about 85 per cent of the total tribal population of the country. The north-eastern states account for the remaining fifteen per cent. They occupy around 18.7 per cent of the total geographical area of the country, usually in the harsh and hostile terrain in the hilly regions and forest areas. The term tribe is derived from the Latin word 'tribus' meaning the 'poor or the masses.' In English, the word 'tribe' appeared in the sixteenth century and denoted a community of persons claiming descent from a common ancestor. The tribal communities of India vary extensively in their 'degrees of isolation, levels of acculturation, numbers and ethnography'. There are about 705 tribal communities in India speaking 105 languages and another 225 secondary dialects.

Odisha occupies a unique position among the Indian states and union territories for having a rich and abundant tribal population. It is considered to have the largest tribal population in India after undivided Madhya Pradesh. There are a number of different tribal groups spreading throughout the districts of Koraput, Rayagada, Malkanagiri, Nabarangapur, Kandhamal, Gajapati, Keonjhar, Sundargarh, Mayurbhanja, Sambalpur, Bolangir, Kalahandi and Dhenkanal. Important tribes include the Kandha, Ganda, Santhal, Saora, Sabar, Kolha, Munda, Paraja, Oraon, Kisan, Bhuyan, Bhottada, and Bhatudi. They belong to different linguistic groups, practise diverse religions and are at different levels of socio-economic condition.

According to the 2001 Census, 118 of the total 314 blocks in Odisha are considered tribal blocks. The estimated tribal population is about 81 lakhs. This is roughly about 22.2 per cent of the state's total population and 9.66 per cent of the total tribal population of our country. 5.1 per cent of the tribal population resides in urban areas, compared to 13.7 per cent for the population as a whole. In the tribal population, 49.9 per cent are males and 50.1 per cent are females, the ratio being 1,003 females per 1000 males. This serves as a significant positive contrast to the corresponding figures for the general population of 982 females per 1,000 males in Odisha. Linguistically, the tribes of India are broadly classified into four categories, namely (1) Indo-Aryan speakers, (2) Dravidian speakers, (3) Tibeto-Burmese speakers, and (4) Austric speakers. In Odisha, the speakers of the Tibeto-Burmese language family are absent, and therefore Odishan tribes belong to other three language families. The tribes of Odisha though belong to three linguistic divisions, yet they have lots of socio-cultural similarities between them. These commonalities signify homogeneity of their cultures and together they characterise the notion or concept of 'tribalism'.

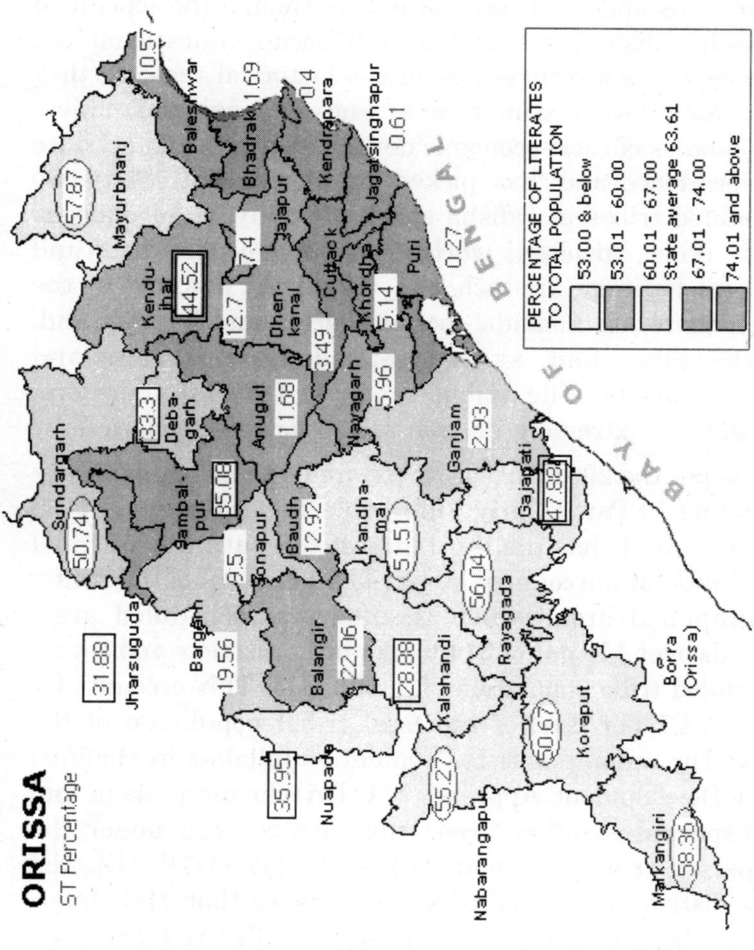

Source: Maps of India

Majority of scheduled tribes live in hilly and forest regions and live differently because of their unique history, culture, ancestry, beliefs, and ways of life. Their knowledge of plants, animals and ways to survive led them to hold wise ideas about how to relate to Mother Earth. Their economy is largely 'subsistence oriented', unorganised and non-specialised. Their social system is simple, and their aspirations and needs are not many. Though the scheduled tribes in Odisha have suffered from social, educational and economic backwardness due to geo-historical reasons, they have their own distinctiveness and socio-cultural milieu. The process of socio-economic development is going on since Independence and 'has picked up momentum'. Sixty-two scheduled tribes in Odisha speak as many as 74 dialects. Their ethos, ideology, worldview, value-orientations and cultural heritage are rich and varied. At one end of the scale, there are nomadic food gatherers and hunters and, at the other end, skilled settled agriculturists and horticulturists. The tribal areas of Odisha, therefore, present an extremely diverse socio-economic panorama.

As per the 2001 Census, there are 62 tribal communities including 13 Particularly Vulnerable Tribal Groups (PTGs) in the state. It has the third largest concentration of tribal population in the country. About 44.70 per cent of the state's geographical area, which is known as scheduled area, extends over 118 out of 314 blocks in 12 districts and covers scheduled tribe population of 3, 398, 343. This accounts for about 54.7 per cent of the total tribal population of the state. The remaining tribal population inhabits in Modified Area Development Approach (MADA)/cluster pockets and is dispersed in other areas that are covered under the Dispersed Tribal Development Programme (DTDP). District wise distribution of ST population shows that Malkangiri district has the highest proportion of STs (57.4 per cent) followed by Mayurbhanj (56.6 per cent), Rayagada (55.8 per cent) and Nabarangapur (55 per cent). The rate of literacy among the scheduled tribes is 37.37 per cent against the overall literacy rate of 63.08 per cent of the state as per the 2001 census. The tribal male and female literacy rates are 51.48 and 23.37 per cent, respectively. Over the last decade, there has been a significant improvement in literacy level among the STs in the state, which recorded an increase from 22.31 per cent in 1991 to 37.37 per cent in 2001.

Almost one-third of India's mother tongues (574 languages) belong to the Indo-Aryan family and is spoken by 73.30 per cent of Indians. The Dravidian languages, 153 in number, form the second major linguistic group of the country (24.47 per cent). There are also separate families like Andamanese that include quite a few diverse languages. Linguists today estimate that one-fifth of India's linguistic heritage may have reached the stage of extinction over the last half-century.

Officially, the Indian State recognises 22 major languages in what is known as the 'Eighth Schedule' of its Constitution (hence, they are officially known as scheduled languages). These languages are also the major literary languages. They are Sanskrit, Assamese, Bangla, Bodo, Dogri, Gujarati, Hindi, Kashmiri, Kannada, Konkani, Maithili, Malayalam, Manipuri, Marathi, Nepali, Odia, Punjabi, Tamil, Telugu, Santhali, Sindhi, and Urdu. No doubt, 'linguistic diversity is a hallmark of India.' (Bhatia and Ritchie, 2004).

An HRD Ministry report says that there are different theories about how many mother-tongues qualify to be called independent languages. "Even Sir George Grierson's 12-volume *Linguistic Survey of India (1903-1923)* – material for which was collected in the last decade of the 19th century – had identified 179 languages and 544 dialects. One of the early census reports also showed 188 languages and 49 dialects (1921 census). Out of these mother tongues, 184 (census 1991) or at least 112 (census 1981 figure) had more than 10,000 speakers. There are other estimates that would put the number higher or lower..." While all languages may have a rich oral tradition, less than half have made the transition to the realm of literacy and formal education. "This may be partly because several tribal languages are still to be formally recognised by state governments in the domain of education, and also, perhaps, because like the policy makers, some groups within the communities themselves are not too convinced about the need to do so, and among those who are convinced, very few know how to put it into practice. Although education in the mother tongue is considered a right in the Indian Constitution, and education is multilingual, tribal mother tongues are still striving for authentic space," says Rajesh Sachdeva, Director of Central Institute of Indian Languages (CIIL), Mysore.

There are only 69-72 languages that are taught in schools in India in some capacity, but radio networks beam programmes in 146 languages and dialects across the country. The highest literary awards in the country are given in 24 languages by the Sahitya Akademi, but newspapers and periodicals, some 3,592 in number, are published in 35 Indian languages every year, the HRD ministry says. Linguists say that determining what should be called a language or a dialect is more a political than a linguistic decision. Most often, the language tag is applied to a standardised and prestigious form, recognised as such over a large geographic area, whereas dialect is generally used to describe the various forms of speech that lack prestige or are restricted to certain regions or communities. Sometimes, mutual intelligibility becomes a criterion; for example, if speakers of Hindi, Urdu and Punjabi can understand each other, they are mistakenly seen as speaking the same language although they may be speaking different languages/dialects.

Adding to this general misperception are the bilingualism figures returned by census reports since 1931. During the 1931 Census, each individual was asked to name any language other than the mother tongue that he/she commonly used. In 1991, a conscious decision was taken to ask for two subsidiary languages rather than one, to get the trilingual figures. India's national average of bilingualism, according to the 1991 Census, turned out to be 19.44 per cent, which was significantly higher than the previous national averages of 9.7 per cent in 1961, 13.04 per cent in 1971 and 13.44 per cent in 1981. Moreover, the average trilingual rate was 7.26 per cent.

The noted writer-activist Ganesh Devy, in connection to this, has clear concerns of his own, "In the census report of 1961, a total of 1652 mother tongues were mentioned. Several hundreds of these are no longer traceable. During the first half of the twentieth century, India reportedly lost about one-fifth of its languages. During the second half of the last century, we have lost about one-third of the remaining languages. If we continue to allow the dwindling of the *bhashas* at this rate, it is estimated that over the next 50 years, we will see the extinction of most of the *bhashas* spoken by the nomadic communities and *Adivasis*, just as we will witness a large-scale erosion of some of the main *bhashas* that have a rich history of written literature."

In Odisha, the speakers of the Tibeto-Burmese language family are absent, and therefore Odisha tribes belong to the other three language families. The Indo-Aryan language family in Odisha includes Desia, Matia, Bhulia, Jharia, Sounti, Laria, Aghria, Kurmi, etc. The Munda (Austroasiatic) language family includes eighteen tribal languages, namely, Gata, Koda, Korwa, Bhumija, Khadia, Mahili, Birhor, Mirdha-Khadia, Ollar, Gadaba, Juang, Bondo, Didayee, Karmali, Santali, Munda, Ho and Saora. And within the Dravidian language family there are nine languages in Odisha, namely, Pengo, Gondi, Kisan, Konda, Koya, Parji, Kui, Kuvi and Kudukh or Oraon. The tribes of Odisha though belong to the three linguistic divisions, yet they have lots of socio-cultural similarities between them.

The languages of each group are inter-related both genetically and structurally. They may be schematically depicted as under (Mahapatra, 1997):

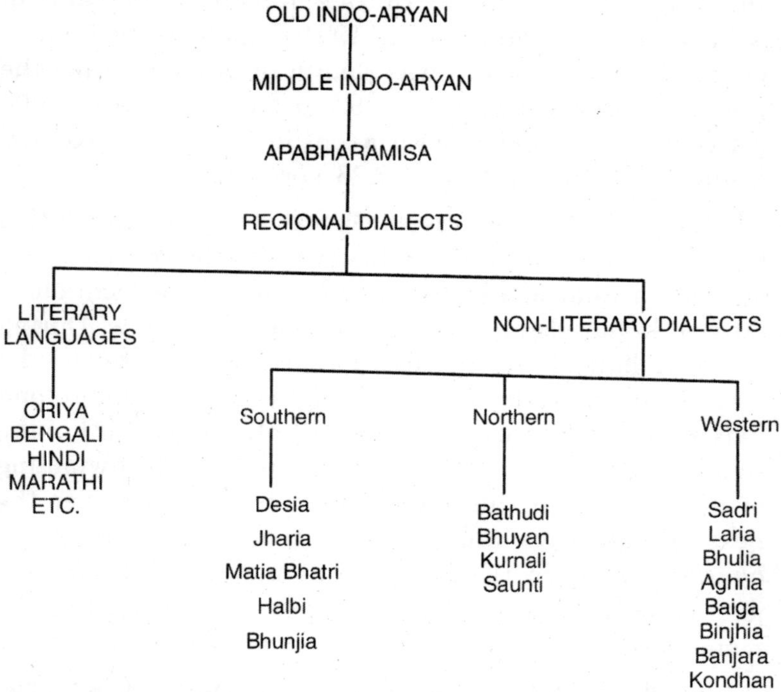

Mahapatra (1997) in this connection says that "all these non-literary Indo-Aryan dialects are used by the tribals either as mother-tongue or second language. These dialects are based on archaic forms of the modern literary languages and have developed peculiarities in the course of time due to convergence of languages belonging to different families, diffusion of linguistic traits across genetic boundaries and hybridisation of language as a result of extensive bilingualism or multilingualism. In multi-familial and multi-dialectal situations, there has been lot of intermixture and mutual borrowing resulting in development of certain common traits among the dialects of divergent origins." They may be schematically depicted as under (Mahapatra, 1997):

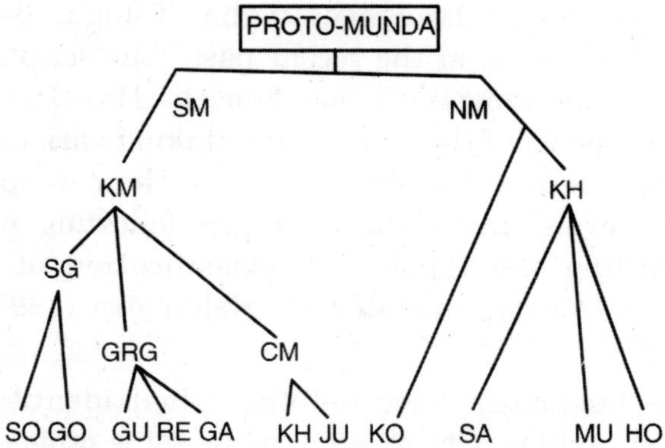

SM South Munda, NM-North Munda, KM-Koraput Munda, CM-Central Munda, SG-Sora, Gorum, GRG-Gutob: Remo; Gta, KH-Kharia, JU-Juang, KO-Korku, KH-Khawari, SA-Santali-(Mahili) Birhor), MU-Mundari (Bhumija, Munda) HO-Kolha)

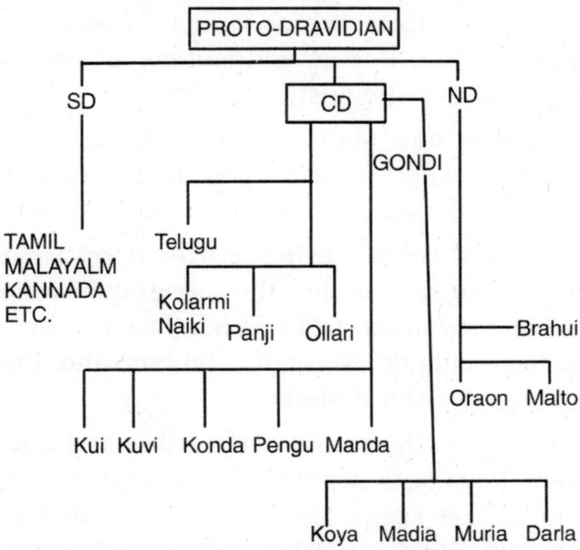

SD-South Dravidian, CD-Central Dravidian, ND-North Dravidian

In general, experts suggest that tribal languages are non-literary (Mahapatra, 1997; Nayak, 1997). The languages began to appear in written form only in the last century. Initially, the Christian missionaries produced written and printed texts in the Roman script. Subsequently, attempts were made for using the scripts of the regional literary languages (Odia, Telugu, Bengali, Hindi, etc.). However, in the recent past, four scripts have been devised for languages like Santali, Ho, Saora and Kui. The exponents of these scripts are taking various steps to promote literacy in the scripts at their respective community levels. In this context, the following notable facts regarding the typological classification of tribal languages of Odisha, as stated by Mahapatra (1997), are to be noted:

- Some languages have definite tribal identity (e.g. Santali, Bonda. Oraon, etc.), while some others have no particular community affiliation but function at inter-community level as lingua franca (e.g. Desia, Sadri, etc.).
- Some of the tribes such as Lodha, Mirdha, Bhumia, Jatapu, Bagata, Pentia, and sections of Gond do not have distinctive linguistic identity.
- Some tribes like Mahali, Kondh, Kisạn, etc., have only dialectical distinction from autonomous languages like Santali, Kui-kuvi, Kudukh, etc.
- Some of the tribes having scattered settlements in different regions under the same tribe-name use different languages, (e.g., Kondh, Saora, etc., living elsewhere outside Koraput, Ganjam and Phulbani districts use Odia dialects).
- In some cases, the names of the tribes and the names of their languages are different (e.g. Dharuas speak Parji, Kolhas speak Ho, Gadabas speak Gutob or Ollari and Kondhs speak Kui/Kuvi or Konda).
- Larger tribes like Kondh, Saora, etc., have several subgroups as ther are Desua/Kutia/Dongria/Pengo/ Jatapu Kondhs and Lanjia/Juray/Arsi/Sudha Saoras and each of these sub-groups speaks a distinct dialect of the languages.
- Languages form cognate groups having much

commonality at the grammatical level and in vocabulary.

The districts of Odisha in which the major eight tribal languages are mostly spoken are indicated below:

Sl. No.	*Language*	*Tribal Districts*
1.	Santali	Mayurbhanja
2.	Sadri	Sundargarh, Jharsuguda
3.	Munda	Mayurbhanja, Keonjhar, Sundargarh
4.	Kui	Kandhamal, Kalahandi
5.	Kuvi	Rayagada
6.	Koya	Malkangiri
7.	Saora	Ganjam, Gajapati
8.	Desia	Koraput, Nawarangpur, Malkangiri

Source: Odisha Information Commission.

Brief Overview of Odisha's Tribal Life

About 44.70 per cent of the area of the state has been notified as the Scheduled Area in accordance with the orders of the President of India, issued under paragraph 6 of the Fifth Schedule to the Constitution. The Scheduled Area in Odisha comprises the entire districts of Mayurbhanj, Koraput (undivided), Sundargarh, Kandhamal, Balliguda and G. Udayagiri Tahsils of Phulbani district, R. Udayagiri Tahsil, Gumna and Rayagada blocks, Soroda Tahsil, excluding Gazalbadi and Gochha Panchayats of Ganjam district, Kuchinda Tahsil of Sambalpur district, Telkoi, Keonjahar, Champua and Barbil Tahsils of Keonjahr district, Th. Rampur and Lanjigarh blocks of Kalahandi district and Nilgiri block of Balasore district. A scheduled district is one where the tribal population is more than 50 per cent of the total population of the place.

The Government of Odisha has adopted the Tribal Sub-Plan strategy since the beginning of the Fifth Five Year Plan (1974-75), which continues to shape the core strategy for tribal development. This strategy is based on area development approach with adequate emphasis on family-oriented income generating activities taking a comprehensive view of tribal problems with the objective of narrowing down the gap in socio-economic development between tribals and others, within the framework of our country's Five Year Plans. The Tribal Sub-Plan (TSP) approach envisages integrated development of the tribal areas, wherein all programmes, irrespective of their sources of funding, operate in unison to achieve the common goal of bringing the area at par with the rest of the state and to improve the quality of life of the tribals. The original strategy was oriented towards taking-up family oriented income generating schemes in the sphere of agriculture, horticulture, animal husbandry, elimination of exploitation, human resources development through education and training programmes and infrastructure development programmes. This tribal development strategy has been reoriented to cover the employment-cum-income generation activities thereto. The strategies more or less continue with refinement over the years, with greater emphasis on tribal development.

Accordingly as per the decision of the government, steps have been taken to impart teaching in tribal languages, i.e., in Santali, Saora, Munda, Bonda, Kui, Kuvi, Juang, Koya, Kisan and Oraon in primary sections of some schools of the SC and ST Development Department of Government of Odisha, which are located in the most remote tribal areas. The Tribal language teachers have been engaged in the schools selected for imparting teaching in the local tribal languages on contractual basis. Rs. 74.00 lakhs have been received from the Government of India, Ministry of Tribal Affairs, under Article 275(1) of Constitution of India in the year 2008-2009 and 2009-010 for remuneration of tribal language teachers. However, this is what has been offered to the public as a matter of statistics. The real situation could be vastly different from what is being professed by the government websites and reports. As per UNICEF figures Odisha has the highest percentage of out-of-school children in the ages six and 14 in India. Therefore the gap existing between the facts and the ground reality is something that needs to be addressed with immediate concerns.

In the last decades, numerous studies have been conducted on the tribal heartland of Odisha. Anthropologists, sociologists, historians, missionaries, reporters, government agencies, tourists, politicians have all, from time to time, tried to penetrate the mystery surrounding the *Adivasis* (original settlers) of Odisha (Kundu, 1994; Mahapatra, 1997; Mishra, 1997; K. Mahapatra, 1998; Zide, 1997; Ghosh, 2003; Pasayat, 2003). What these seekers have brought to light is far more fascinating than fiction. Indian literature is also richer today with the addition of notable works from eminent writers like, W. G. Archer (*The Blue Grove,* 1943, *The Hill of Flutes,* 1974), Verrier Elwin (*Tribal Myths of Orissa,* 1954, *Leaves from the Jungle,*1992), Hem Barua (*The Red River and the Blue Hill*, 1954) Gopinath Mohanty (*Paraja,*1945 *Amrutara Santana,* 1947), Sitakant Mahapatra (*The Endless Weave,* 1991, *Unending Rythms*, 1992), Maheswata Devi (*Byadhkhanda,* 1994) and Pratibha Ray (*Adibhumi,* 1993), who have incisively portrayed the trials and tribulations of the tribal world in their books. No doubt, the tribal population of Odisha is primarily concerned with the struggle for survival. It is constantly troubled by drought, near famine conditions, poverty, etc. Yet it has much to teach us. Each tribe is a completely organised society, bound by a common language, religion, cultural background and tradition, all in all a way of life. These tribes definitely represent an earlier stage in the development of man. Of all the states of India, Odisha has the largest number of tribes, as many as 62. Altogether, they constitute an impressive 23 per cent of the total population of Odisha. These tribes mainly inhabit the Eastern Ghat hill range that runs in the north-south direction. More than half their population is concentrated in three districts – Koraput, Sundargarh and Mayurbhanj.

Tribal economy is 'subsistence oriented'. It is based on food gathering, hunting and fishing and thus revolves around forests. Even the larger tribes like the Santal, Munda, Oraon and Gond, who are settled agriculturists, often supplement their economy with hunting and gathering. While farming, they make use of very simple technology and simple division of labour, often limited to the immediate family. They lose out because their holdings are small and unproductive, lacking in irrigation facilities since the terrain is hilly and undulating. They also lack funds to buy other inputs and necessarily fall back upon traditional skills and outdated implements. Many tribes, for instance, the Juang, Bhuyan, Saora Dharua and Bondo, practise what is called shifting cultivation, also known as slash and burn. They select a plot of land, generally on a mountain slope, slash down all the trees and bushes and burn them to ashes. Spreading the ashes evenly over the land, they wait for the rains before planting their crops. Two or three seasons on one plot of land and the soil is depleted, so the tribals move on. It is a way of life for them, but a harmful practice just the same, bringing poor returns and degrading the environment in the bargain.

There are cattle breeders among the tribes, notably the Koya. There are simple artisans too like the Mohali and Loharas, who practise crafts of basket weaving and tool making. A sizable part of the tribal population of Odisha has moved to the mining and industrial belts of the state, notably the Santals, Munda, Oraon and Ho. This has helped ease the pressure on small holdings, but in the process, tribal villages have been abandoned. Traditional skills, land and other immovable assets have been lost without always bringing in adequate prosperity via jobs in mines and factories. However, if tribal economy is shaky, tribal culture in its virgin state is rich and distinctive and the *Adivasis* work hard to preserve it. A tribal village manages its internal affairs very smoothly through two institutions – the village council of elders and the youth dormitory.

The core of tribal culture, the youth dormitory, is the largest hut in the village. It has only three walls, generously decorated with symbols representing animals. The fourth side is open. By night, the dormitory is home to the youth of the village. Generally, before and after a hard day's work, people gather here to chat and relax. The council of elders meets here, too, to discuss matters relating to the welfare of the village. The open space in front of the dormitory is where the young people sing and dance with gay abandon every evening, for tribal culture allows free mixing of the two sexes. Despite their poverty and the on-going battle for survival, the tribals of Odisha have retained their rich and vibrant heritage of dance and music. Every tribal can sing and dance to the sound of pipe and drum and give tune to spontaneous compositions that come to him quite naturally. But, today maybe things are changing gradually as young people prefer to dance and sing to the tunes of popular songs from Hindi, Odia and other dominant languages.

The tribals of Odisha observe a string of festivals. Some are close family concerns, relating to a birth or death within the family or a daughter attaining puberty. Others relate to sowing or harvest time and thus involve the entire community. Mostly a festival is an occasion for liberal consumption of *handia* (rice beer) and *mahua* liquor, consumption of meat and a night of song and dance and revelry. Sometimes, there are animal sacrifices too, for the deities and spirits are thought to be appeased first, particularly the 'malevolent' ones, so they do not unleash drought or disease on the land. Tribals are superstitious people and the *ojha* (witch doctor) occupies a position of honour since he not only prescribes medicines for the sick but is also believed to exorcise evil spirits. The supernatural figures prominently in tribal folklore, which is largely a body of oral literary traditions (Mahapatra, 1993). These simple folk tales are linked to occasions in everyday life – sowing, harvesting, birth, marriage and death. Folk tales also teach values dear to the tribal heart. However, many of them explain natural phenomena like day and night, thunderstorms, animal behaviours, etc. With the tribals living so close to nature, it is all but natural. Christian missionaries in the last few years have done a lot to remove superstition from tribal societies, educating tribals and setting them on the road to economic stability. The numerous missionary educational institutions and organisations are proof of this. But in the process, they have also converted many to Christianity. Religious distribution figures for tribals of Odisha as per Census 2001 shows 88.2 per cent Hindus, 7.4 per cent Christians and 4.5 per cent in the other religion categories. The OTDP (Odisha Tribal Development Programme) is also working to bring the benefits of development to the area. Much still remains to be done, but development must not override the tribal way of life. It would be a great pity if due to modernisation we cease to retain this rich and meaningful way of life that has come down to us from antiquity.

The Study Area

Sundargarh district, situated on the north-western part of the state, was constituted on 1st January, 1948 out of the two ex-States of Gangpur and Bonai, which merged with Odisha on that day. True to its name, this 'beautiful' district of Sundargarh with about 43 per cent of its total area under forest cover and numerous colourful tribes dotting its landscape and with abundant mining potential is bounded by Ranchi district of Jharkhand on the north, Raigarh district of Chhatisgarh on the west and north-west, Jharsuguda, Sambalpur and Angul districts of Odisha on the south and south-east and Singhbhum district of Jharkhand and Keonjhar district of Odisha on the east. Geographically, the district is not a compact unit and consists of widely dissimilar tracts of expansive and open countryside dotted with tree-clad isolated peaks, vast inaccessible forests, extensive river valleys and mountainous terrains. Broadly speaking, it is an undulating tableland of different elevations broken up by rugged hill ranges and cut up by torrential hill streams and the rivers Ib and Brahmani. Mainly four tribes, namely, the Mundas, the Oraons, the Kisans, and the Khadias are the indigenous tribes of the place, and form the majority of the tribal population of the district.

Sundargarh District at a Glance

1. Topography:

1.	Topographic Location	Latitude - 21°36′N to 22°32′N Longitude- 83°32′E to 85°22′E
2.	Geographical Area	9712 sq kms (Second largest district in the state accounting for 6.23 per cent of the total area)
3.	Normal Rainfall	1657.1 mm
4.	Forest Cover	4232.57 sq kms (Second largest in the state accounting for 8.53 per cent of the state total)
5.	Major Rivers	Brahmani Sankh and Koel – Tributary of Brahmani Ib-Tributary of Mahanadi
6.	Major Soil Type	Alluvial and Lateritic

2. Demography (As per 2001 Census)

1.	Population	1830673
2.	Density	188 (2001) per sq km
3.	ST	918903
4.	SC	157745

3. Socio-Economic Features

1.	Cultivated Land	3,36,000 Hects
	High	1,86,000 Hects
	Medium	95,000 Hects
	Low	55,000 Hects
2.	No. of Cultivators	1,97,019
3.	No. of Agricultural Labourers	91,068
4.	Average Size of Operational Holdings	1.73 Hects
5.	Class-wise Number of Operational Holdings	
	Class	Number
	Marginal	65,281
	Small	51,767
	Semi-medium	35,696
	Medium	12,279
	Large	984
	TOTAL	1,66,007
6.	Per Capita Availability of Foodgrains	155 kg/year
7.	Cattle Population	17,36,327
	Buffaloes	60,929
	Cows	2,84,939
	Bullocks	6,76,121
	Sheep/Goats	7,14,338

4. Administrative and Legislative Units

1.	No. of Sub-divisions	3
2.	No. of Tehsils	16
3.	No. of CD Blocks	17
4.	No. of GPs	262
5.	No. of Villages	1744 (Inhabited – 1688) (Uninhabited-56)
6.	No. of Urban Local Bodies	4
7.	No. of Fast Developing Urban Pockets	5
8.	No. of Parliamentary Constituency	1
	No. of Assembly Constituencies	7

5. Literacy Rate

1.	Total	18,22,42	65.22 per cent
2.	Males	9,34,902	75.69 per cent
3.	Females	8,94,510	54.25 per cent

Source: sundergarh.nic.in

The Bonai sub-division of the district is more mountainous and forested than other parts and it is here that the hill Bhuyans, the most primitive tribal community, inhabits. This subdivision is marked by some of the high mountain ranges, which form the important physical features of the topography of the district. One of the hill ranges is Bichakani (2964 ft.), which has rich iron-ore deposits. This deposit feeds the Rourkela Steel Plant of Steel Authority of India Ltd. (SAIL) that is situated right in the heart of the tribal belt of the district.

A new era in the Indian steel industry was heralded when the construction work on one of India's three first public sector steel plants was started in October 1956 at Rourkela, situated in the Panposh subdivision of

Sundargarh district. It is one of the most modern and largest steel plants of the Steel Authority of India Limited (SAIL), built under Indo-German collaboration. The transformation of Rourkela from a cluster of hamlets inhabited by the *Adivasis* to a modern and cosmopolitan township is a symbol of the industrial development of India. Rourkela has the privilege of housing one of Asia's most modern steel plants whose annual production capacity at present is 4.5 million tonnes of hot metal, 4.2 million tonnes of crude steel and 3.99 million tonnes of saleable steel.

Girdled by verdant hills, surrounded by three rivers, the modern steel township has come up at Rourkela where not long ago existed an inhospitable thick forest full of wild life, and inhabited by a variety of primitive tribes such as the Mundas, the Oraons, the Kisans, and the Khadias. Spread over an area of 48 square kilometres, the township is divided into sectors on the two sides of the beautiful two-way ring road. The mega steel works on one side of the hill range and the comfortable residential accommodation in picturesque setting, asphalt roads, adequate educational, medical and recreational facilities which are amply provided in the township. On the other side of the hill range is an unique symbol of Indo-German friendship, and stand as a remarkable success of industrial development in the midst of an area inhabited by the tribal communities who reflect an age-old civilisation, representing a linguistic diversity that is perhaps not easily matched by any other place in the world. One of the objectives of such a study is also to find out the extent of interaction between these two strata of society that represent almost the two extremes. The name 'Rourkela' means 'Our Village', derived from *Rour* which means 'our' and *kela* means 'village' in the local Sadri language spoken by various tribal communities living here in the city. It is the lingua franca adopted by all the tribal groups of the city.

Present Tribal Language Situation in Sundargarh District of Odisha

The main language that is spoken in Sundargarh district is locally known as Sundargadi, which is a form of the Sambalpuri language ("http://en.wikipedia.org/wiki/Sambalpuri_Language"). People of Aghria community who migrated to Odisha, specifically to western Odisha, from Agra (hence the name), in north India, in search of a better life, speak the Aghria language. The Aghria community is a relatively well-off peasant community who are placed as an 'interface between upper-caste and tribal societies'. At present, they are listed under the Other Backward Caste (OBC) category in the Government of Odisha caste hierarchy list. In village areas of Sundargarh that borders Jharsuguda district of Odisha and Raigarh district of Chhattisgarh, the main language is Aghria, as most of the total population is Aghria. The tribals of Sundargarh district largely speak Mundari, Kudukh, Khadia, Kisan, Binjia and Santali languages as their mother tongues. Santali is written in Ol Chiki script. Like Odia language, Santali language is also specified in the Eighth Schedule of the Constitution of India. Every year, an All India test is held in Santali language which is equivalent to the 10th class examination. But Santali is not an indigenous Sundargarh tribal language. It is mainly spoken in Balasore, Bhadrak, Mayurbhanj, Keonjhar and Dhenkanal districts of Odisha. People who speak Santali in Sundargarh district have basically migrated to this place for job purposes. Sadri language is the lingua franca among tribal people of this district. Ironically, compared to other tribal languages of the area, Sadri is positioned much better in the respectability scale by the tribals themselves and hence is thriving in the township areas, at least for the current period. Hindi is also widely understood and spoken by people of the district due to its close proximity with Jharkhand and Chhattisgarh. Due to its cosmopolitan character, people of Rourkela use standard Odia or standard Hindi as medium of communication. However, English and Odia languages are used for all official purposes.

The Sadri Language

Sadri is a branch of Prakrit language and is regarded as a sister language of Odia, Bengali and Angika. It is spoken in the Indian states of Jharkhand, Odisha and the north of West Bengal, and in Bangladesh. While the Chero tribe of Uttar Pradesh and Bihar use Sadri as their first language, it has also become a lingua franca of all Jharkhandi tribal communities. Besides speaking their own mother tongues, the Oraon, Kisan, Munda, Bhuyan, Mahali and Khadia communities speak in Sadri with each other in many parts of Jharkhand, Odisha, Chhattisgarh, north Bengal, Assam, Andaman and Nicobar, and other parts of India, where Jharkhandi communities reside. Most of the people of the Oraon, Munda and Khadia communities along with the Kisan, Bhuyan, and Gond group that constitute the tribal communities of Sundargarh and Rourkela, today speak it as their first language. Sadri language plays a cementing role among the various tribes of the tribal communities of Rourkela. While the Oraons, Gonds, Bhuyans, Mahalis and Kisans form a part of the Dravidian linguistic family, the Mundas and Khadias belong to the Austric linguistic family.

Statement of the Problem

As an aftereffect of industrialisation and modernisation, local indigenous languages like Sadri, Munda, Khadia, Kudukh (Oraon), Kisan, etc., belonging to Rourkela and its nearby town areas along with other small towns and villages of Sundargarh district, are regularly exposed to the languages of the migrant population. These migrants come from all over India and majority of who speak English, Hindi and Odia. The cosmopolitan culture of Rourkela city has been bolstered by the use of multiple number of languages. Gradually, from a Munda, Sadri and Kudukh dominated place, this place has been transformed into a Hindi/Odia dominated zone. Today, English has also made rapid inroads into the vocabulary of these indigenous people, exactly as it has happened for their more affluent co-habitants from the non-tribal communities.

Education, which is the cornerstone of any development, ironically has been a major contributor in the gradual non-use of indigenous languages by the younger generation. The young generations are getting their primary and secondary education in the dominant languages of the state, that is Odia, Hindi and English, and hence do not seem too interested to practise their own native tongues. Because of the linguistic and economic restructuring of the place, folk/ tribal culture, literature and language is facing an identity crisis today, and is unable to withstand the challenges of a rapidly developing techno-urban Rourkela. In addition, there is also a major perception among people that public education in regional languages is a disadvantage vis-à-vis education in English, and thus more and more people from the lower strata are forced to seek expensive English-medium private schools for their children. 'Over the post-Independence years, English has become the single most important predictor of socio-economic mobility' (Mohanty, 2004).

According to government reports, a total area of more than 30,000 acres of lush green tribal land has been acquired until now for setting up the Rourkela Steel Plant and the Steel Township, Railway Lines, Fertiliser Township and the subsequent Mandira Dam Project of Rourkela Steel Plant. The Rourkela ripple effect can also be seen in other parts of Sundargarh district, which in recent years has attracted ample investments in industrial and mining activities due to its rich mineral resources. Some tribals have found employment in these industrial installations and there have been heightened economic activities in the area that has helped the tribals financially and socially.

Language endangerment is the culmination of complex internal and external pressures that induce a speech community to adopt a language spoken by others (Crystal, 2000). These may include changes in values, rituals, social, economic and political life resulting from trade, migration, intermarriage, religious conversion, military conquest or because of development in the name of industrialisation. Along with the accompanying loss of culture, language loss can destroy a sense of self-worth, limiting human potential and complicating efforts to solve other problems, such as poverty, family breakdown, school failure and substance abuse. After all, language death does not happen in privileged communities. It happens to the 'dispossessed and the disempowered' people who most need their cultural resources to survive (Crystal, 2000). Many minority communities associate their disadvantaged social and economic position with their ancestral culture and language. They have come to believe that their languages are of no use anymore and not worth retaining. Speakers of minority languages abandon their languages and cultures in the hope of overcoming discrimination, to secure a better livelihood and enhance social mobility for themselves and their children. 'India is a multilingual country in which many languages coexist, many languages are maintained, but at the same time, many languages are also treated with neglect, discrimination and deprivation. In practice, Indian multilingualism is characterised by unequal status of the languages' (Mohanty, 2004). The reasons for this kind of hierarchical setting among languages is the 'sense that some languages are privileged with access to power and resources while others are disadvantaged due to various forms of neglect' (Mohanty, 2004).

Experts have maintained that endangered languages are not necessarily languages with few speakers (Krauss, 1992; Crystal, 2000). Even though small communities are more vulnerable to external threats, the size of a group does not always matter. The viability of a language is determined primarily by the general attitude of its speakers towards their heritage culture, of which their language may be considered the most important component. In this respect, the intergenerational transmission of the language, i.e., teaching the children the heritage language, is the most important feature of language vitality. But it is being seen more and more that today's younger generation, due to the impact of urbanisation and to a certain extent due to the influence of popular culture (TV, cinema, internet, music, computer, video games, etc.) is moving away from their own culture and language and trying to adopt the culture and language of the dominant community. The need to assimilate into a so-called 'superior' culture is so high that the younger generation is readily agreeing to forgo their age-old traditions and culture, which ironically has given them their unique identity. This effect is being seen even on a 'safe' language like Odia, so the effect on tribal languages of Odisha can very well be gauged from this. According to Krauss (1992), as many as half of the estimated 6,000 languages spoken on earth are 'moribund', that is, they are spoken only by adults who no longer teach them to the next generation.

The 2001 Census of India has 6641 raw returns of mother-tongues and they have been further rationalised into 1635 mother tongues and 1957 names which are treated as 'unclassified' and relegated to 'other' mother tongue category. The 1635 mother-tongues are further rationalised into 122 mother tongues by following the usual linguistic methods for rational grouping based on available linguistic information, and grouped under 22 Scheduled languages and 100 Non-scheduled languages. The census report also states that mother tongues having a population of less than 10000 on all-India basis, or, were not possible to identify on the basis of available linguistic information, have gone under 'others'. Therefore, as per the latest census report, a good number of 'languages' recorded in the Indian Census could not be classified as to their genetic relation, and so are treated as unclassified languages. Officially, some 310 languages are counted as 'endangered' in India. Among them, some 10 languages spoken by more than 1,000 speakers are said to have a better chance of survival. These include Adibhasha, Bakerwali, Beldari, Jatapu, Kanjari, Raj, Sarodi, Sohali, Subba, Tirguli, besides some others like Bare, Kolhati, Khasal, Inkari and Uchai that are spoken by close to 1,000 speakers. But there are 47 others claimed by much less than 1,000 speakers and 263 more returned during the census by less than five speakers that are difficult to verify.

In 1971, data from the census was distributed in two categories, the officially listed languages of the Eighth Schedule, and the other languages with a minimum of 10,000 speakers each. All other languages spoken by less than 10,000 speakers were lumped together in a single entry: 'Others.' This practice continues to be followed and as linguist Uday Narayan Singh comments, "The problem with Indian labels is that the 1961 Census had floated so many mother tongue labels (1,652), especially among the unclassified languages (the 'others'), that it will have to be worked out as to how many of them finally survived – which is itself a gigantic task." However debatable the methodology followed by the Indian census, particularly the 1961 Census, linguists and activists conclude that a fifth of India's linguistic heritage may have reached the stage of extinction over the last half-century.

Taking into account all the fundamental issues involved in a project of such nature, the study was conducted with the following key objectives in mind:

Research Objectives

- To examine the extent to which English and major Indian languages have affected the tribal languages of western Odisha.
- To study the level of decline, if any, of these tribal

languages and to assess the future positioning of these languages in the society as a whole.

- To amass data on actual language practice in the interior parts of western Odisha, covering the tribal dominated Sundargarh district, in order that policy makers in this area can be better informed.

Thus the study attempts to answer the following important questions:

Research Questions

- How far English and dominant state languages have influenced the tribal languages of north-west Odisha, with special focus on the once dominant languages of Sundargarh district like Munda, Khadia, Kudukh (Oraon), Kisan, Sadri, etc.
- Are these tribal languages on a path of decline and what does the future hold for such tribal languages of India?
- Why do people from subordinate cultures and languages not take enough effort or adequate measures to preserve their culture and language?

Definition of Terms

The following terms have associated meanings in the research study undertaken:

Modernisation

Taylor (2001) defines modernity as a set of changes in institutions and practices—the development of a dynamic, market-oriented industrial economy, a bureaucratically organised state, organised military forces, and (in some versions) modes of stable popular rule. The first three changes, if not the fourth, are in a sense irresistible. Whoever fails to adopt them, or some functional equivalent, will fall so far behind in the power stakes as to be conquered and forced to undergo these changes anyway. This definition of modernisation has been accepted in the study concerned.

Tribals

In the present study, the term tribals refer to the indigenous groups of people who share a common name, speak a common language, occupy or profess to occupy a common territory and are not usually endogamous though originally they might have been so (Patnaik, 2002).

Tribal Identity

The tribal people express their cultural identity and distinctiveness in their social organisation, language, rituals and festivals and also in their dress, ornaments, art and craft (Mohanty, 2004). Yet, at one extreme, are the groups that lead a relatively isolated and antiquated way of life, keeping their culture intact, while at the other extreme, there are communities that are indistinguishable from the general agricultural communities.

Language Identity

Language is one of the most important indicators of the tribal identity (Devy, 2002). The language of each community is unique and distinct and the speaker of that language owns allegiance to that particular language community. Identifying with one's own community being a strong marker of their distinctiveness, language becomes a significant vehicle for identification among the tribals.

Language Endangerment

A situation where a language is spoken by enough people to make survival a possibility, but only in favourable circumstances and with a growth in community support (Crystal, 2002). Crystal (2002) goes on to add that that endangered languages have few or no children learning the language, and the youngest good speakers are young adults.

Language Shift

Language shift happens during cultural assimilation. A socially and economically strong language community, because of social, political and economic reasons, can inadvertently force the disadvantaged group to own allegiance to the dominant language because of perceived superiority of the language and community.

Language Death

A language is said to be dead when no one speaks it any more (Crystal, 2000). It may exist in the recorded form but unless there are people who actually speak the language it cannot be called as a living language. Complex language contact situations between dominant languages and indigenous languages result in language loss or language death of the lesser languages.

Significance of the Study

Perhaps nowhere else in the world is the problem of language endangerment as great as in India, but unfortunately, very little effort is being made to protect these languages. Also, it is an established fact that minority languages, particularly tribal languages, are more prone to extinction. Modern cultures, encouraged by emerging technologies and widespread industrialisation, are rapidly intruding into the lives of these once-isolated people with drastic effects on their way of life and on the environment, they inhabit. Destruction of lands and livelihoods, spread of consumerism and Western values, pressures of assimilation into dominant cultures, and deliberate policies of repression directed at indigenous groups – these are among the 'factors threatening the world's biodiversity as well as its cultural and linguistic diversity.' David Crystal, the noted linguist, in his book *Language Death* (2000; pp. 93), has used the term 'preventive linguistics' to describe the branch of linguistics which provides information about the world's endangered languages and enables linguists and policy makers to take steps to preserve them or even to revitalise them. According to Crystal, "Half the languages of the world are likely to die out in the next 100 years -

and if this happens, it would be a true intellectual disaster. The world is a mosaic of visions, expressed through language. If even one language is lost, it is awful."

Preservation of our tribal languages become essential not only for the survival of our ancient cultures, but it also plays an important role in providing information on the values, beliefs and understanding of a person's origin. All languages change and are changing at different rates and in different ways (Zide, 1997). However, giving up a mother-tongue, i.e., not just learning a second or third language, but completely dropping the mother-tongue is a serious matter. Psychologically and emotionally, much of one's basic emotional repertory is embedded in the mother-tongue. Therefore, allowing a mother-tongue to die, particularly in a country as linguistically diverse as India is nothing less than a crime against humanity. It may be administratively simpler for many of us, but it is damaging and traumatic to those people who are at the receiving end of such callousness showed by the people who matter and who have the power to bring in a qualitative difference in the lives of these vulnerable communities of India.

Industrialisation, no doubt, brings in faster growth of national income, alleviation of poverty, and reduction of income inequalities, leading to an improved quality of life in general. Without industrial development, and its by-product urbanisation, the whole world would still be in the dark ages, but a development that embraces the inclusive growth of all the stakeholders is hardly seen in the Indian context. A major case in point is the recent confusion and controversy surrounding the Vedanta Resources group, which, as per newspaper reports, disregarded all norms in trying to mine bauxite on a forested hill considered sacred by the ancient Dongria Kondh tribe of Kalahandi district of Odisha. The tribes of Odisha have their distinct ethnic identity, which is clearly marked in their languages besides many other cultural traits and traditions. Tribal Odisha in fact represents a micro-linguistic area as three different ethnic and linguistic communities divided into sixty-two separate tribes live here together scattered throughout the state. In this context, a survey of the various language situations has become indispensable for forming a clear picture of the inherent language related problems of the people and the area and for taking policy decisions that would facilitate in preserving our linguistic diversity for posterity.

As language constitutes an integral part of society and individual's identity, people's attitudes towards it must have strong effects on its status within a given community. Gardener and Lambert's (1972) study of language attitude, commonly accepted as systematic attempts in the field of language teaching and learning, proposes motivation as a construct made up of specific attitudes to language. The most important of these is group-specific; the attitude learners have towards the members of the cultural group whose language they are learning. In this context, we can say that a tribal speaker's positive attitude towards Hindi, Odia and English languages would build a strong motivation in him to learn these languages. In such cases, the language learner is said to have 'integrative motivation.' Other learners may be interested in learning a language just because they want to achieve certain objectives through it. These are believed to have 'instrumental motivation'. It is this kind of motivation that plays an increasing role in leading the tribal populace of the area to learn the dominant languages in the host environment.

According to Mahapatra (1997), many tribals view their own tribal languages as unsuitable for use in official domains. They believe that these languages lack the capacity for expressing ideas in a variety of domains. As a result, indigenous languages have been excluded from all aspects of communication in official settings. The neglect experienced by these languages played a significant role in creating a negative attitude towards them, which is today invariably leading to their demise. To counter this situation, language revival strategies and procedures are urgently needed. As most tribal languages are found only in oral form, proper documentation and recording could be of great help in preserving the languages. A documented language potentially receives the power to create, reproduce and advertise itself in a new way. A non-documented language, on the other hand, tends to maintain only a local essence and existence (Adegbija, 1992).

Limitations of the Study

Precision of any study depends upon the accuracy and reliability of data and their sources and the methodological approach followed. All studies therefore are subjected to errors and few limitations. The findings of the present study are subjected to the following limitations:

- The study area was confined to few tribal villages and towns in Sundargarh district. Thus the results of the study are applicable only to similar kind of situation analysis.
- The study pertained to the economic year 2008-2009.The result may not be completely valid for over a longer period of time due to fast changing socio-economic setting in the study area.
- The findings of the study are based on the ground situations prevailing within the Odisha context and hence cannot be generalised fully.

Concluding Remarks

Languages of the world need to be preserved. They are the routes to safeguard our traditional knowledge and traditional cultural expressions. When languages become endangered, a way of life becomes endangered, leading to a serious loss of identity. Therefore, to begin with, proper information on languages, which are facing threats from dominant languages of the place, need to be elicited so that appropriate measures can be formulated for documentation and preservation. Without concrete evidence of the endangerment level of the language, it becomes difficult for the policy-makers and administrators to devise measures for countering the threat situation. Thus, this becomes the responsibility of scholars and researchers of tribal languages to study and disseminate the information for the knowledge of a wider public.

2
Situating Language Impact and Language Endangerment in the Tribal Context

This chapter is divided into two sections. The first section reports the prior studies that have investigated language contact and language shift in different parts of the world and in India. It thus reports the prior studies that have investigated the impact of dominant languages on minority languages in a worldwide context. The second section discusses the importance of preserving endangered languages, how languages get endangered, who are the people who are affected by this endangerment and why this should be a universal concern and what should be the focus of a concerned society while trying to preserve the world's language diversity.

Section–I: Language Impact in the Context of Minority Languages

Since long, there have been serious debates among sociologists and anthropologists regarding a proper definition of tribals. By the nineteenth century, a tribe came to be seen not only as part of a particular society, but also a particular stage of evolution. A 'tribe' was often defined as an isolated, self-contained and primitive social formation (Pati, 2011). Generally, the terms tribe/tribal/ tribalism have been used as labels by anthropologists to designate groups regarded as pre-modern, non-literate or primitive (Mahapatra and Dash, 1996). Often scholars consider the term 'tribe' as a derogatory one and mention it as synonymous with aborigines and indigenous people (Mahapatra and Dash, 1996; Dash, 1996). Yet, in the Indian context, the term 'tribal' is too complex to be a synonym for 'indigenous' (Devy, 2002). All throughout India's long and chequered history, communities have migrated, evicted, displaced and then again resettled. Devy (2002) suggests that since it is impossible to typify tribals by any single characteristic feature, in the present-day context, 'tribals are simply the most underprivileged or underdeveloped groups in the country.' Therefore, given the difficulty in defining the tribal identity, we have to go by the government-notified definition for Scheduled Tribes (ST), which mentions that STs are those, which are notified by the President of India under article 342 of the Constitution. The first notification was made in the year 1950. The President considers characteristics like the tribe's primitive traits, distinctive culture, shyness with the public at large, geographical location, and social and economic backwardness before notifying them as scheduled tribes. However, Devy (2002) is of the opinion that anyone experienced in tribal society and culture will find these definitions to be overtly simplified. Therefore, 'the most useful indicator of tribal identity is their language.'

The review of related literature of language impact of perceived major languages on relatively minor languages brings to light the fact that the threat to linguistic resources is now recognised as a worldwide crisis. According to Krauss, as many as half of the estimated 6,000 languages spoken on earth are 'moribund', that is, only adults who no longer teach them to the next generation speak them.

According to a study by population biologist Bill Sutherland of the University of East Anglia in the United Kingdom, published in *Nature,* 90 per cent of the world's

6809 living languages are spoken by fewer than 100,000 people; 46 of them have only one native speaker left. 'Rare languages are more likely to show evidence of decline than commoner ones,' said Professor Sutherland. He has demonstrated that languages are subject to the forces of extinction similar to those of biological species, though language extinction seems to occur at more than double the rate of species extinction: over the last five centuries, 4.5 per cent of described languages have disappeared, compared to 1.3 per cent of birds and 1.9 per cent of mammals.

Èerný (2010) is of the opinion that reasons for language loss (and/or language shift towards a stronger language, frequently English) are numerous. Besides natural disasters (earthquakes, hurricanes, tsunamis, etc.), colonisation, migration, and invasion, often resulting in cultural assimilation, or even genocide, can also be mentioned.

Dorais (1995) suggests that when people are faced with a choice between a dominant business language and a traditional language they always lean towards using the dominant, intruding language, even when they appreciate that their local language is significant to their contemporary, cultural, collective identity - that is, to the way they perceive and define their own place in the world. That was one of the findings of Louis-Jacques Dorais in his studies on language attitudes and behaviours in the early 90s in Canada's Eastern Arctic, in Igloolik, Nunavut, and Quaqtaq, Nunavik.

Elias (2008) is of the view that the transition from a local traditional indigenous language in which one feels at home, to a dominating language and culture that embraces modernity involves a redefinition of the self. There is an 'irresistible force' on ethnic speakers and cultures to identify as moderns and to deny their ethnic identities, the languages of business and commerce are adopted and languages that express a different world view 'become secondary or are abandoned.' Yet, as research has shown (Cerný, 2010), language revival is often successful. And, as Crystal (2002) points out the reasons why we should safeguard our languages, 'we need diversity, because languages express identity, because languages are repositories of history, because languages contribute to the sum of human knowledge, because languages are interesting in themselves.'

In this context, we can cite Fishman's (1991) theory that delineates four social changes affecting our language choices: (1) demographic factors, (2) economic forces, (3) social identifiers, and (4) mass media. Additionally, Fishman (1991) proposed a graded division of languages according to their endangerment (for details, see Fig. 1). As the following figure suggests, Stage One languages are the least threatened, with higher levels of government and educational institutions using the language. Stage Eight languages, on the contrary, are most seriously endangered, having only a few speakers left. The remaining six stages rank between these two ends:

Table 2.1: Adaptation of Fishman's Scale for Threatened Languages

Stage One - Used by higher levels of government and in higher education.
Stage Two - Used by local government and the mass media in the community.
Stage Three - Used in business and by employees in less specialised work areas.
Stage Four - Language is required in elementary schools.
Stage Five - Language is still very much alive and used in community.
Stage Six - Some intergenerational use of language.
Stage Seven - Only adults beyond child bearing age speak the language.
Stage Eight - Only a few elders speak the language.

Crystal (2000) again opines that "comparing levels of language endangerment is very difficult, in view of the diversity of language situations around the world, and the lack of theoretical models which would allow us to interpret combination of relevant variables." Rhydwen (1998) in this connection provides a most relevant perspective, "Loss of language is not the loss of a concept, an abstraction, but rather it is what happens when people change their behaviour and stop transmitting their language intergenerationally." Aitchison (1981) believes that when a language dies, it is not because a community has forgotten how to speak, but because another language has gradually ousted the old one as the dominant language, for political and social reasons. For linguists like Claude Hagege, languages are not simply a collection of words. They are living, breathing organisms holding the connections and associations that define a culture. When a language becomes extinct, the culture in which it lived is lost too.

In the Odishan tribal context, studies (Devy, 2002; Mahapatra, 1973; Mahapatra, 1993; K. Mahapatra, 1997) show that this is exactly the problem with most of our tribal languages. Mahapatra (2004) in his study, *Tribal Languages of Odisha*, found out that Bonda, Oraon have definite tribal identity; whereas languages like Desia, Sadri, etc., have no particular community affiliation but function at inter-community level as lingua franca. According to him, "Tribal ethnography can never be complete without reference to their verbal behaviour. The most fundamental characteristics of human verbal behaviour are preserved in their languages which are distinctively observed in vocabulary, sound symbolism, grammatical structures or such other aspects."

Mohanty (2004) in his paper, 'Tribal Culture in Odisha', states that "the tribal people express their cultural identity and distinctiveness in their social organisation, language, rituals and festivals and also in their dress, ornaments, art and craft." Srivastava (1984) provided a new approach towards defining minority-majority languages based on two principles, 'quantum' and 'power.' Pandharipande (2002) states that, according to this view, a language can be of four types: (a) powerful as well as majority (e.g. Marathi in Maharashtra); (b) powerless but majority (e.g. Kashmiri in Jammu and Kashmir); (c) minority but powerful (English in all the states); (d) minority and powerless (tribal languages in all the states).

Mohanty (1994) and Mohanty and Parida (1993) have surveyed the attitude towards maintenance of own language and culture and out-group relationship in bilingual and monolingual tribal-nontribal contact areas, to find out the role of contact bilingualism in intergroup relationship. They studied Kond adult villagers (from the monolingual and bilingual areas combined). In the bilingual contact areas, the Konds and the non-tribals showed a mutually integrative relationship and maintenance orientation. Thus, stable bilingualism in contact situations seems to be associated with positive intergroup relationship. On the other hand, language shift (resulting in monolingualism for the minority group) is associated with the assimilative attitude of minority groups. Thus, this study of language and culture contact shows that the Konds are a minority contact group which has clearly accepted its minor and minority status vis-à-vis the other language and culture in contact.

Annamalai (2001) in his book, *Managing Multilingualism in India: Political and Linguistic Manifestation*, says, "Tribal languages can be maintained only if these are promoted, developed and used for administrative and educational purposes." The National Policy of Education (1986) has given special place to education of the scheduled tribes. It emphasises on the need to develop the curricula and devise instructional materials in tribal languages at the initial stages with arrangements for switching over to the regional languages. The statement given by the first Prime Minister of India, Pandit Jawaharlal Nehru, on June 1, 1960 in the Conference on *Tribes and Scheduled Areas* at New Delhi, can be mentioned here, in this context, as it holds true even after over five decades have passed by in the meantime: "The language problem is almost always exceedingly important from the psychological point of view. The best solutions one might offer would break down if it produced wrong reaction on the other side. One must make it perfectly and absolutely clear that government would encourage the tribal languages. It is not a question of merely allowing them to continue. They must be encouraged and helped and made to flourish."

Mishra (1997) observes that ethnic identity is maintained through the language, rituals, customs, food, dress, manners, speech, dance, music and such other aspects of culture of a particular ethnic group, which distinguish them from others. More specifically, the oral traditions of each ethnic group bear the ethnic characteristics, manifested through language, symbol and cultural objectives. Hence if languages are allowed to die, a whole culture and a way of life dies with it.

Section – II: Language Endangerment and the Need for Preserving Indigenous Languages

There are quite a few theoretical approaches in understanding the ethno-linguistic identity and attitudes in language contact situations. In inter-cultural research, Berry's (Berry, 1990; Berry and Sam, 1997) model of cultural relations in plural societies has been widely used to understand the outcomes of cultural and linguistic contact. This model analyses the contact outcomes in terms of acculturation attitudes of individuals and communities in contact along two dimensions—maintenance of one's own identity, culture, language and the way of life ("own group maintenance and development", Berry, 2003), and establishing and maintaining a positive relationship with the other group ("other group acceptance and tolerance", Berry, 2003). Depending upon positive or negative attitudes with respect to these two dimensions, Berry's model identifies four outcomes; assimilation, integration, separation and marginalisation (deculturation). Although the concept of deculturation/marginalisation in the model has been questioned (Del Pilar and Udasco, 2004), the model is extensively used and empirically supported (Berry and Sam, 1997) in inter-cultural research.

"Why should we save our languages? And for whom should we save them?" Vaharu Sonawane, a revolutionary *Adivasi* poet from remote Nandurbar district in north-west Maharashtra, enquired in the Bharat Bhasa Confluence, held in April 2010 at Ahemedabad, India. "We are told that every time two people converse, a language is born. In addition, every time a particular conversation ends, a language dies. Therefore, languages die around us all the time. Then what is this fuss all about?" Vaharu, who writes in Marathi and Bhilodi, his mother tongue, has formulated his own logic to satisfy the query he raises. He believes the basis of the 'variety' in human culture today was laid in the *Adivasi* condition over 10,000 years ago, before humans discovered agriculture. The population of those involved in agriculture increased gradually and they became a majority. Very few *Adivasi* communities accepted the agriculture system. And even if some of them got into agriculture, they maintained their varied and unique traditions.

Thus, according to Vaharu, the 'main treasury' of the variety of human cultures and traditions was maintained outside of agriculture by the *Adivasis* in Africa, Asia, America and elsewhere. It was maintained throughout their independent existence as also in their enslavement and exploitation. The different *Adivasi* cultures and traditions, evolved over several centuries, have many things worth keeping. If the *Adivasis* lose their speech, all of it will be lost because the heart of a culture or tradition is voice. "That is why, it is important we save our languages. And we save them for the whole of humanity, as also our own future generations," Vaharu concludes.

In the same conference, O.C. Handa, a renowned scholar in history and archaeology of the Himalayan region, said something similar in a different context and on another subject: "Sanskrit is hardly spoken now, but it lives on in many other languages. It has enriched so many languages spoken today in our country. Similarly, Sanskrit might have enriched itself by borrowing from other languages spoken in ancient India. I am not worried about the origin of a language or whether it lives or dies. That is a part of the social process. Whether languages benefit the common people should be the real concern." Professor Chandrakala Rawat from Himachal Pradesh agrees with Vaharu, but says that in the Himalayan region, where dialects change every four kilometres, Hindi has come to dominate as the main communication link. "We are taught Hindi from the primary-school level. There is no place for our mother tongues, Kumauni or Garhwali, despite each having several thousand speakers. Imagine the plight of other minor languages with fewer speakers. Things have come to such a pass that mothers in our area beat up their children if they hear them speaking Kumauni or Garhwali. 'Speak Hindi/English or you will remain illiterate like us,' our future generations are told. Now, how do we save our languages?"

Writer-activist Ganesh Devy feels it is time for all to act: "Aphasia, or loss of speech, seems to be our collective fate. Aphasia is being imposed on all of us. It is a daunting task to determine which languages have come closest to the condition of aphasia, which ones are decidedly moving in that direction and which ones are merely going through the natural linguistic process of transmigration. But let us ensure that all the 320 languages represented at the Bharat

Bhasha Confluence 2010 will live on."

Ramnika Gupta of the Ramnika Foundation in Jharkhand says many languages spoken by *Adivasis* and *Dalits* in the country are endangered because of government policies, particularly in education, as well as the constant external cultural assault via television, films and the constant presence of media of all kinds in 'mainstream' languages. "There are some 600 tribes in India of which around 75 are found outside the northeast and, barring a few, nearly all of them have either lost their language already or are on the verge of losing it. In most cases, they have been subsumed by the language of the majority," says the octogenarian who publishes the voices of *Adivasi* and *Dalit* writers across India through her foundation's 'All India Tribal Literary Forum' (AITLF).

Eminent linguist and the founder-director of the Central Institute of Indian Languages (CIIL), Mysore, D P Pattanayak (1990), believes that all Indian languages are threatened. "It is not only the small tribal languages, but even major languages like Hindi and Odia. We are witnessing a situation where English is at the top while some 35 Indian languages are at the bottom. The smaller languages are facing a double threat from English and major Indian languages like Hindi." Linguists argue that although Indians speak different languages, they are repeating the same ideas. That is, if we are speaking a kind of Hindi that is merely a translation of English and expresses only ideas borrowed from the West, it is not Hindi. It may also be the other way around resulting in 'Hinglish'. "This is more than a question of intrusion of foreign words. We seem to be losing touch with all that shaped our languages historically and culturally," Pattanayak says.

According to a report on the website of the Union Human Resources Development (HRD) ministry: "Having recognised the importance of English as an instrument of knowledge dissemination as well as commerce as well as maintenance of international relations, a provision was left to extend the use of English language in the Article 343 on 'Official language of the Union' – for all the official purposes of the Union' even after 'a period of fifteen years', with a proviso that 'the President may, during the said period, by order authorise the use of the Hindi language in addition to the English language and of the Devanagari form of numerals for any of the official purposes of the Union."

"India is a peculiar case," says Rajesh Sachdeva, present director of CIIL. "Nobody knows how many languages are spoken in the country. But India is essentially a multilingual country where linguistic diversity is part of the historical cultural heritage and an integral part of nation building philosophy. This provides both a challenge and an opportunity."

"In speech communities such as Marathi, Gujarati, Kannada and Odia, the younger generations have little or no contact with the written heritage of those languages, though they are able to 'speak' the languages as 'native speakers'. It may not be inappropriate to assume that people all over the world are paying a heavy price for a globalised development in terms of their language heritage. This linguistic condition may be described as 'partial language acquisition' in which a fully literate person, with a relatively high degree of education, is able to read, write and speak a language other than her/his mother tongue, but is able to only speak but not write the language she/he claims as the mother tongue," Devy observes.

The reorganisation of Indian states after Independence has been carried out along linguistic lines. The languages that had not acquired scripts did not have printed literature and hence did not get their own states. Schools and colleges were established only for the official languages. The ones without scripts, even if they had oral traditions, did not get educational institutions. Yet the current success on the part of language activists in keeping languages like Bhilli or Santali alive is not shared by other marginalised languages like Mundari in Odisha/Jharkhand, Bhilodi in Maharashtra, Gondi in Chhatttisgarh, Karbi in Assam, or Kandha in Odisha, just a few of those currently fighting for official recognition. This, linguists say, is to the detriment of the country as a whole. "Each of these languages, which could not flourish beyond their speakers' areas due to lack of scope for wider use at the national level, is endowed with the potential to add something to our national integration," says Dr. Deviprasad Shastry, head of the Tribal and Endangered Languages Department at the Central Institute of Indian Languages, Mysore.

Language Maintenance and Tribal Identity

Rogers (1959) believed that humans have one basic motive, that is the tendency to self-actualise—i.e., to fulfill one's potential and achieve the highest level of 'human-beingness' we can. Like a flower that will grow to its full potential if the conditions are right, but which is constrained by its environment, so people will flourish and reach their potential if their environment is good enough. Rogers was of the opinion that for a person to 'grow', an environment is needed that provided him with genuineness (openness and self-disclosure), acceptance (being seen with unconditional positive regard), and empathy (being listened to and understood). If we put this in the context of modernisation and tribal identity then it is seen that in the recent years loss of their indigenous cultural identity has been the fallout of development.

Tribal identity defines and locates an individual within itself and within the larger context of the world, providing a framework in which humans can depend on to interact with each other and the natural environment (Thomason, 1999). The loss of that tribal identity has meant the loss of ritual and a consistent value system which humans have depended on for stability and sense of security. "No longer identifying with a tribe has fragmented the conceptual framework we use to make sense of the world and give life meaning. A sense of direction and purpose is diminished or harder to perceive, as is our place in the world and our understanding of what it means to be human" (Thomason, 1999).

In India, Verrier Elwin, in 1943 proposed a new trend in ethno-methodology in which it was suggested that tribals should be kept isolated in their hills and forests. Elwin's theory is known in Social Anthropology as 'Public Park Theory'. He suggested that ordinarily the non-tribal people should not be allowed to enter into tribal pockets without permission of the state government. This system would guarantee the isolation of the tribals. Majumdar (1944) differed marginally from this view. He agreed with the position that the cultural identity of the tribals should be retained as far as possible. He feared that if the isolation was broken the tribals would lose their ethnic identity. But he was in favour of 'selected integration' of the tribals. He proposed that not all the elements of civilisation should be allowed to enter the tribal area. Only those which have relevance with tribal life should be permitted into such area. Such a policy would keep the tribals away from the 'vices of urban life.'

Bose (1977) has provided some insight into the social life of the tribal. "Tribes differ from others in their social system. They have retained their own marriage regulation. Almost all marry within their restricted local group, and are sometimes guided by their own elders or political chief in internal and external affairs. In other words, they form socially distinct communities who have been designated as tribes and listed in the Schedule for special treatment, so that within a relatively short time they can come within the mainstream of political and economic life if India."

Xaxa (2005) observes that the overall thrust of the Indian Constitution towards tribes is one of integration rather than assimilation. Although the meaning of integration may be understood in different ways, the underlying assumption is that it provides space for diversity, unlike assimilation, which extends no such space. The conception of assimilation entails that the small minority must give up its culture in favour of the dominant majority. Therefore, the aim of all our policies and practices should be towards integration and not assimilation, as is mostly seen in the Indian context.

Mahapatra (2001) is of the opinion that tribal languages and literatures of our country constitute an invaluable part of our national literary heritage. Their lack of script does not mean they lack excellence or complexities in expression. Their oral traditions contain valuable song-poems, legends, tales and riddles that deserve to be documented, and that also quickly because with rapid socio-economic transformation these run the risk of dying away or getting distorted and forgotten.

Pattanayak (1990) offers a solution to this language maintenance problem by suggesting that the tribal children should be taught in their mother-tongues. "To think that they do not have languages and speak only in dialects undermines their self-confidence. If multilingual education is based on the language which the child knows, speak and understands, while moving into reading and writing she comes to know the rule governed character of the language. She comes to understand the difference between the spoken and written styles of a language and also between one language and another. His imagination is stirred, creatively challenged and knowledge is enhanced."

It is important to note that many of these languages have survived being overwhelmed down by mainstream languages and cultures because of their rich oral traditions. Today, it is believed that there is more scope for survival because of the rise of literacy among the various speech communities. Languages will never die until the speakers abandon them. Language loss and linguistic shifts cannot be blamed on globalisation forces and government policies alone. "The overpowering desire among parents to educate their children in English, along with French and German as second languages in place of the mother tongue, to make them more productive labour for international markets, is equally to blame," says Professor Rawat.

Before she died early this year at the age of 85, Boa Senior, the last speaker of the Bo-language - one of the ten Great Andamanese languages - spent her days speaking to birds on the faraway islands. "She would simply look at the skies and keep talking to the birds and then smile and say it was the only way she could keep her language alive," Anvita Abbi, the well-known linguist from Jawaharlal Nehru University, New Delhi, recalls. In India nobody noticed the death of the language that dated as far back as 65,000 years, until Professor Abbi announced it and the Western media picked up the news (*New Indian Express*, 2012). Boa Senior's death was a loss for intellectuals around the world wanting to study more about the origins of ancient languages and one of the oldest tribes of the Great Andamanese, who now number just 52. Originally, 10 distinct tribes, the Great Andamanese were 5,000-strong when the British colonised the Andaman Islands in 1858. Most were killed or died of diseases brought by the colonisers. Most of the Great Andamanese tribes have forgotten their mother tongues and speak in Hindi now. Even Boa Senior had to learn an Andamanese version of Hindi in order to communicate with her own people.

Professor Abbi is concerned about the future of languages spoken by the Andamanese tribes. "The extinction of a language is unnatural because languages never die. Our native languages have survived the onslaught of Sanskrit, English and Hindi for centuries," she says. Writer-activist Ganesh Devy is worried that, like Boa Sr and her language Bo, there are many other languages in the country on the verge of extinction. "How can you sit and watch when so many people are faced with the global phonocide (combining the Greek word 'phonetics' with the Latin word 'cide' or killing) let loose in our times?" he asks.

Pattanayak hopes the central government will gather 'enough courage' to conduct a linguistic survey, long overdue in the country "because that is the only way to know all our languages...I am sorry about the linguistic survey [not being conducted earlier by the government]. We do not care about the tribals. There is nothing about them in our history, geography and social sciences." The Linguistic Survey of India (LSI) had planned an official survey, touting it as the biggest ever such exercise conducted in the world, in April 2007. The survey was to be conducted by the CIIL. Rajesh Sachdeva, director of CIIL, who was present at the Bhasha Confluence, said the exercise had to be abandoned with "the government developing cold feet".

Governments for the past several decades have feared that linguistic surveys could lead to *bhasha-vaad* or language disputes in a country where states were formed on linguistic lines. But Sachdeva feels India has come a long way since Independence, "*Bhasha chintan ka, chinta ka masla nahin hona chahiye* (Language should be a subject for reflection, not for social tension)." He conceded that accurate information on the number of languages, especially smaller languages, spoken in the country, was the need of the hour. "Though Grierson's survey inspired a large number of studies on language, it also had some drawbacks. It excluded the former province of Madras and the then princely States of Hyderabad and Mysore from its purview. As a result, nobody knows exactly how many languages are spoken in India," Sachdeva said.

G.N. Devy, the noted linguist, has also expressed concern that "while our cities have become 'Bhasha Bharat' (drawn from the Mahabharat) with the migration of speakers of different languages, we did not prepare them for this situation, leading to many social problems." The situation he was referring to was the language wars in Maharashtra, where, incidentally, language diversity is more than anywhere in the country with some 209 languages. West Bengal and Gujarat follow with around 150 languages spoken in each state, while Delhi is next with a language diversity of 120.

Sandwiched between government apathy and the growing need to be a part of the dominant culture, the tribals of Odisha are fast losing touch with their mother-tongues. The state's rich repository of tribal languages is depleting fast. This has happened despite the government's stand vis-à-vis tribals and the need to preserve their dialects. While states like Madhya Pradesh, Maharashtra, Rajasthan and West Bengal have come out with a tribal-friendly language policy, Odisha has no clear-cut language policy so far. As a result, only 25 tribal groups — of the total 62 — have survived the onslaught of foreign languages and retained their own dialects. The rest have gradually come to accept Odia as their mother-tongue.

The education scenario itself speaks volumes about the state government's apathy to preserve tribal languages. A news report in *The Indian Express* dated December 26, 2002, titled "Tribal dialects dying in Odisha", by Shyamhari Chakra, states that none of the tribal dialects is taught in schools, leave aside their use as a medium of teaching. The lone experiment to introduce a tribal dialect in the school curriculum was made by the Biju Patnaik Government in the early nineties when C.P. Majhi was education minister. Majhi had introduced a local dialect, Ol Chiki, as a subject in 20 primary schools of Mayurbhanj, Keonjhar and Sundargarh districts. While the government has been apathetic, the communities have hardly fought for their rights to speak their tongue. Most of the efforts by people like Pandit Raghunath Murmu, Mangei Gamang, Dayanidhi

Mallick and Lako Bodhra to develop scripts for Santal, Saora, Kui and Ho communities have not been as effective as it was evinced. Acknowledging the abysmally low tribal literacy percentage and high drop-outs among school children, in recent years the government of Odisha has started a Multilingual Education (MLE) programme, under which tribal children are to be taught in their mother-tongues at the primary level. This programme has already been piloted in several schools across the state, but the effectiveness of the programme is yet to be established.

Concluding Remarks

The literature review thus reveals that even though numerous studies have been conducted regarding tribal language scenario in the worldwide context, and even in the Indian context, not many studies have been done taking into account the western Odishan context. Sundargarh district of Odisha is a Scheduled Area, as declared by the President of India, and the tribal population of the area certainly deserves to have their languages to be protected from other dominant languages, for the benefit of their future generations. The first step towards preservation of our indigenous languages can happen only when proper documentation of the endangerment levels of the languages are conducted by scholars and researchers of languages.

3

Materials and Methods

This chapter presents the methods and procedures that the researcher followed to make the impact assessment of English and major Indian languages on tribal languages of western Odisha, so that appropriate strategy building and policy making could be planned for safekeeping of the minor languages of the state. It also enquires into the reasons why language maintenance is not being considered to be a priority area for the tribals themselves when they are very much aware that their languages and its concomitant, their cultures, are almost on the verge of extinction. It seeks the right medium through which these issues can be addressed and subsequently rectified through major policy interventions. The research design followed a questionnaire-based survey, in addition to unstructured interview method, among the tribal population of the area. The tribals were observed in a natural context, i.e., in their own residences, work places, market places, schools and colleges. The researcher chose a survey research design because it best served to answer the questions and the purposes of the study. The survey research is one in which a group of people or items is studied by collecting and analysing data from only a few people or items considered to be representative of the entire group. In other words, only a part of the population is studied, and findings from this are expected to be generalised to the entire population.

The questionnaire survey conducted in different villages and towns of Sundargarh district are included in this study to ascertain the ground level realities of the acculturation process. The chapter begins with the description of the research subjects (tribals) and research instruments and concludes with a description of the methods and procedures that were followed to analyse the data.

Sample Population

The informants were drawn from a fairly large cross-section of the communities so that representative sample of all the local languages could be studied. Various kinds of settings were undertaken to study the changing attitude, if any, of the informants towards their language since the time industrialisation and urbanisation have happened in Rourkela and Sundargarh district at large. Data collected from the various villages, slums and from the township areas were studied in detail to facilitate a comparative study of language contact and change. Stratified random sampling technique was employed to select the sample population. The sample size consisted of around 900 persons from various age groups of both genders, out of which 355 people belonged to the 5–15 age group, 223 belonged to the 16–30 age group, 182 belonged to the 31–54 age group and 140 people belonged to the above 55 age group. Fifty-eight per cent of the respondents were male, while female respondents constituted 42 per cent.

The tribal people express their cultural identity and distinctiveness in their social organisation, language, rituals and festivals and in their dress, ornaments, art and craft. This study was undertaken to get first-hand knowledge and information on the impact that massive industrialisation and urbanisation have had on the linguistic diversity of the tribal dominated place that Rourkela was once upon a time. The study also includes the other small towns and villages of Sundargarh district, which also face a similar linguistic influence from a few major languages of the country. A study on this 'language contact' scenario would help in recording and maintaining the related data and also facilitate in preserving some of our endangered tribal languages by bringing forth the tragic dichotomies existing in these tribal communities that are corroding their original way of living.

According to Fasold (1987), the methods for determining subjects' attitudes about language can be direct or indirect. A typically direct method requires subjects to state their opinions about a given language in reply to a questionnaire or interview questions that simply ask about their feeling towards a language or another. A very indirect method could be one in which the subjects are unaware of the fact that their language attitude is being tested. Given the relatively big number of the target population, the researcher chose the first method. The study was conducted among both the educated populace of the towns and villages and among the labourer class populace living in various slum areas (*bastis*) of the towns. Around 900 respondents have been accessed from Rourkela, Rajgangpur, Biramitrapur, Panposh, Badgaon, Badmal, Bisra, Bandhamunda, Kutra and Nuagaon divisions of Sundargarh and from Karkatta, Tiklipada, Patrapalli, Lelepada, Khudgaon, Barilpata, Kantajhara and Hatibari villages of Sundargarh district. The data collection process was undertaken from a cross-section of people, along with personal interviews with experts from the related areas.

Instruments of the Study

A questionnaire (Appendix I) based on the various objectives and target areas of the study was prepared and used as the research tool, along with interviews and personal interactions. The questionnaire for eliciting information was prepared based on UNESCO's existing questionnaire on endangered languages accessed from the document on *UNESCO Programme Safeguarding of Endangered Languages,* Paris, 10–12 March 2003, by the UNESCO Ad Hoc Expert Group on Endangered Languages. The researcher, as per the local context and needs, modified the questionnaire. The important parameters included in the survey questionnaire were language use, language maintenance and shift, language identity, language contact, code-switching, attitude towards language use, language status and preservation. The questionnaire was prepared in both English and Odia for better understanding and access during data collection. Both qualitative and quantitative studies were undertaken to assess the reality of the situation. The base data were the various issues and problems experienced by the tribals regarding their ancestral languages within and outside the family and community life. Although the questionnaire was not divided into different stages, each question collected specific information.

Validation of the Questionnaire

The questionnaire designed for the study was subjected to a validation process for face and content validity.

During the validation process of this study, copies of the research questions and copies of the questionnaire were provided to some well-known linguists of the state and a few language experts of the locality. These experts went through the research questions and the questionnaire carefully to ascertain the appropriateness and adequacy of the instrument. The changes and modifications asked for by these experts were then incorporated into the questionnaire to make it better applicable to the local situation and, hence, more suitable and effective for the study undertaken.

Having validated the questionnaire, a pilot testing was carried out on the instrument using 30 persons from each age group accessed from some of the villages of Jharsuguda district of Odisha, which is not the district in which the actual research was supposed to be carried out. This was done in order to observe:

- how the subjects responded to the questionnaire;
- whether the items had enough clarity and were easily understood by the respondents;
- whether there was any need to include more items in certain areas, and whether there were items to which they did not like to respond; and
- to determine the suitability of the suggested method of data analysis for the study.

From the pilot test, the researcher was able to understand the ambiguity of some of the items and hence appropriate modifications were made to bring the instrument to a better comprehensible level.

Administration of the Research Instruments

After the pilot testing and all necessary modifications, the copies of the questionnaire were administered directly to the chosen sample for the study. Nine hundred copies of the questionnaire were given out and were successfully completed and returned. The researcher, along with other research assistants, personally visited the various villages and nearby township areas and conducted the survey. It was conducted during academic year 2009-2010. Administration of the questionnaire was conducted by the researcher over a period of eight months. At the selected research sites, the researcher also got the permission to conduct the survey in the classroom atmosphere, i.e. the study was conducted in various schools and colleges, which helped in collecting data from a large cross-section of the population in a relatively short period of time. A lot of questionnaires had to be filled up by the researcher and her teams, as many of the respondents were illiterate and also many of them were not willing to write down anything. In fact, many of the respondents were quite skeptical of the whole thing. They could not understand why anyone should be interested in their languages. They wanted to know the benefits that would come their way if they spoke about their life and languages. Only the school children and a few educated tribals of the township areas were forthcoming with their answers and observations.

Methods of Data Analysis

The study made use of 900 copies of questionnaire to collect information from the four groups of tribal population of the district. There were 30 questions in the questionnaire covering all the above-mentioned parameters related to language endangerment and maintenance. The questions were framed to conduct an impact assessment of the English language and major Indian languages on the tribal languages of Sundargarh district of Odisha. The questionnaire was prepared in both Odia and English for better understanding of the respondents. The major focus of the questionnaire was on the prevailing language use scenario among the tribals of the place and how far they are interested in taking the effort to preserve their language. In addition to the demographic details, both open and close ended questions related to the given parameters like language use, language maintenance and shift, language identity, language contact, code-switching, attitude towards language use, language status and preservation have been used in the questionnaire. The scoring of the close ended questions (question nos. 4, 5, 6, 8, 9, 11, 12, 13, 14, 15, 16, 17, 18, 20, 21, 22, 23, 24, and 29) is based on summating all the items for each individual to get a raw score for a particular individual. The group data was analysed using the descriptive measures for frequencies and percentages. For the open ended questions (question nos. 7, 9, 10, 25, 26, 27, 28 and 30) qualitative analysis was done to understand the prevailing tribal language scenario of the district.

Four tribal languages, along with Sadri, which is the tribal lingua franca of the area, dominate the Sundargarh-Rourkela zone. The four languages are Oraon, locally called Kudukh, Munda, Khadia and Kisan. Santali and Binjia languages are used by a few tribal families. But since these are not indigenous Sundargarh tribal languages, we limit our study to Sadri and the above-mentioned four dominant tribal languages of the place. The data collected is analysed and presented separately for each language for clarity and easy understanding of the reader. The qualitative analysis was done on the basis of the major evaluative factors of language vitality suggested in the document, entitled, *Language Vitality and Endangerment* submitted to the *International Expert Meeting on UNESCO Programme Safeguarding of Endangered Languages,* Paris, 10–12 March 2003, by the UNESCO Ad Hoc Expert Group on Endangered Languages.

The criteria suggested by the UNESCO experts are furnished underneath for general reference of the reader.

Major Evaluative Factors of Language Vitality Assessment

(1) Intergenerational Language Transmission; (2) Absolute Number of Speakers; (3) Proportion of Speakers within the Total Population; (4) Trends in Existing Language Domains; (5) Response to New Domains and Media; (6) Materials for Language Education and Literacy; (7) Governmental and Institutional Language Attitudes and Policies, Including Official Status and Use; (8) Community

Members' Attitudes towards their own Language; and (9) Amount and Quality of Documentation.

Degree of Endangerment	*Grade*	*Speaker Population*
Safe	5	The language is used by all ages, from children up.
Unsafe	4	The language is used by some children in all domains; it is used by all children in limited domains.
Definitively endangered	3	The language is used mostly by the parental generation and up.
Severely endangered	2	The language is used mostly by the grandparental generation and up.
Critically endangered	1	The language is used mostly by very few speakers, of great-grandparental generation.
Extinct	0	There exists no speaker.

Methods of Statistical Analysis

The group data of all the sections were analysed based on the frequencies and percentages. A schematic representation in the form of bar graphs is produced for all the sections.

4

Results and Discussion

This chapter presents the research findings on an impact assessment of English and major Indian languages on tribal languages of western Odisha conducted through a questionnaire survey, among four groups of tribal population, namely, the Mundas, the Oraons, the Kisans and the Khadias. Independent variables related to the research questions as language endangerment, language identity, language loss, language preservation, code-switching, etc., in a language contact context were taken into consideration. These variables were selected for data analysis which has been described in detail. The responses to the questionnaire (both quantitative and qualitative) were calculated on SPSS 18.0 software. The quantitative data was collected from items 4, 5, 6, 8, 9, 11, 12, 13, 14, 15, 16, 17, 18, 20, 21, 22, 23, 24 and 29 and qualitative data from items 7, 9, 10, 25, 26, 27, 28 and 30. The findings relating to the research questions are discussed in detail. The quantitative data analysis is followed by the qualitative data analysis of the questionnaire. (See Appendix - I for details).

Results Related to Research Questions 1, 2 and 3

The SPSS (Statistical Packages for Social Sciences) package was used to analyse answers to the questions on language attitude and endangerment. Frequency and Chi-square tests were employed in the process.

Table 4.2 shows that 76.13 per cent of the entire population investigated reported that Hindi/Odia/English was their preferred language. This means that indigenous languages are preferred by less than 24 per cent of the respondents. It seems that the predominant role of Hindi/ Odia in the area has decreased positive attitude towards ethnic languages as vernacular-speaking communities actually use more Hindi/Odia than their own languages in most domains of communication.

The table also shows that language preference does not differ significantly from the first to the third group. For the first, second and third groups, a vast majority reported (81.9 per cent) that they preferred to speak Hindi/Odia and English. In other words, less than 19 per cent of the ethnic minority younger generations preferred speaking their ethnic languages. Among the older generation, positive attitude towards ethnic mother tongues was found among 61.11 per cent of the Sadri group, 57.7 per cent of the Munda group, 60 per cent of the Kudukh, 58.9 per cent of the Khadia and 64.28 per cent of the Kisan.

These results, however, when compared to the actual use of language by these people suggest that the extent to which tribal languages are used cannot be taken as evidence for language loyalty among these groups. That is, most minority language communities tend to use the dominant language in the host environment in spite of the fact that they claimed that they preferred to speak their own languages. The general picture indicates a significant tendency to language shift even among vernacular-speaking older generations.

For the initial three groups, the proportion of those preferring to speak Hindi/Odia and English increases to 81.9 per cent. Compared to the fourth group, loyalty to tribal languages decreases to about 18 per cent. From these figures, a significant tendency to language shift towards Hindi/Odia/English can be observed. This suggests that Hindi/Odia/English is being highly valued among younger generation members of ethnic minority groups in western Odisha.

Among the fourth group, the proportion of tribal language preference increases significantly. 60.71 per cent and 39.28 per cent of this group reported that they preferred to speak Hindi/Odia/English and their mother tongues, respectively. However, loyalty to the ethnic languages does not necessarily materialise in people actually speaking the languages in all domains. All the groups are, in fact, highly conscious of their own ethnic and cultural identity. They tend to signal their tribal affiliation by using their tribal languages whenever language choice is available for them in a given context.

The table also shows that in the interview process while strong language loyalty among the language communities was perceived consistently across the different age groups, it proved to be remarkably deceptive when it came to actual language use. This is simply because members of the various language groups are highly conscious of the importance of Hindi/Odia in practical domains such as education, career, business and commerce, social interaction, etc.

Table 4.1: Language Considered Most Important to Master (Respondents in Numbers)

	Age group 1 (5-15)		*Age group 2 (16-30)*		*Age group 3 (31-54)*		*Age group 4 (55 and above)*	
	Hindi/Or/ Eng	*Tribal*	*Hin/ Or/Eng*	*Tribal*	*Hin/Or/ Eng*	*Tribal*	*Hin/Or/ Eng*	*Tribal*
Sadri	95	19	54	8	36	12	22	14
Munda	59	13	43	7	30	11	15	11
Kudukh	56	11	33	7	32	09	18	12
Khadia	44	09	31	6	19	06	20	14
Kisan	42	07	29	5	20	07	09	05
Total	296	59	190	33	137	45	85	55

Table 4.2: Language Considered Most Important to Master (Respondents in Percentage)

	Age group 1 (5-15)		*Age group 2 (16-30)*		*Age group 3 (31-54)*		*Age group 4 (55 & above)*	
	Hindi/Or/ Eng	*Tribal*	*Hin/ Or/Eng*	*Tribal*	*Hin/Or/ Eng*	*Tribal*	*Hin/Or/ Eng*	*Tribal*
Sadri	83.3	16.60	87.09	12.9	75	25	61.11	38.88
Munda	81.94	18.05	86	14	73.7	26.8	57.69	42.3
Kudukh	83.58	16.41	82.5	17.5	78.04	21.95	60	40
Khadia	83.01	16.98	79.48	15.38	76	24	58.8	45.17
Kisan	85.71	14.28	85.29	14.7	74.07	25	64.28	35.71
Total	83.38	16.61	85.20	14.79	75.27	24.72	60.71	39.28

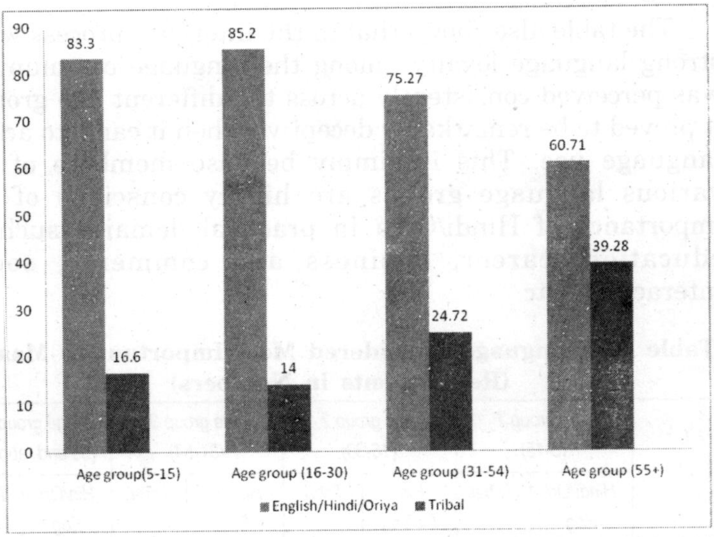

Fig. 4.1: Language Considered more Important to Master

Parents' Language Preference for Children

In this section, we will investigate the languages that tribal group members like their children to learn. Such an analysis will give a clear picture of the future of tribal languages in western Odisha. This is because if parents find it necessary for children to learn the group's language, they will spare no efforts in achieving this goal and consequently chances of tribal languages surviving the onslaught of dominant state languages will be higher. Tables 4.3 and 4.4 give the distribution of languages that respondents prefer for their children to learn and speak.

Table 4.3: Language Considered Most Important for Children to Learn (In Absolute Numbers)

	Age group 2 (16-30)		*Age group 3 (31-54)*		*Age group 4 (55 and above)*	
	Hindi/Odia/Eng	*Tribal*	*Hindi/Odia/Eng*	*Tribal*	*Hindi/Or/Eng*	*Tribal*
Sadri	54	8	36	12	16	20
Munda	43	7	30	11	11	15
Kudukh	33	7	32	09	12	18
Khadia	31	6	21	04	14	20
Kisan	29	5	22	05	06	08
Total	190	33	141	41	59	81

Table 4.4: Language Considered Most Important for Children to Learn (In Percentage)

	Age group 2 (16-30)		*Age group 3 (31-54)*		*Age group 4 (55 and above)*	
	Hindi/Odia/Eng	*Tribal*	*Hindi/Odia/Eng*	*Tribal*	*Hindi/Or/Eng*	*Tribal*
Sadri	87	13	75	25	44	66
Munda	86	14	73.17	26.8	42.3	57.6
Kudukh	82.5	17.5	78.04	21.9	40	60
Khadia	83.78	16.22	80.7	19.2	41.17	58.8
Kisan	85.29	14.7	81.48	18.5	42.85	57.14
Total	85.2	14.7	77.47	22.5	42.14	57.85

Table 4.4 shows that 85.2 per cent of the second age group reported that they liked to see their children speak the dominant languages of the place. Preference of local indigenous languages, on the other hand, was found among 14.7 per cent of the respondents. The figures suggest that about 85 per cent of the age group did not see learning of tribal languages as a top priority for their children. The table also shows that parents from the Sadri group reported

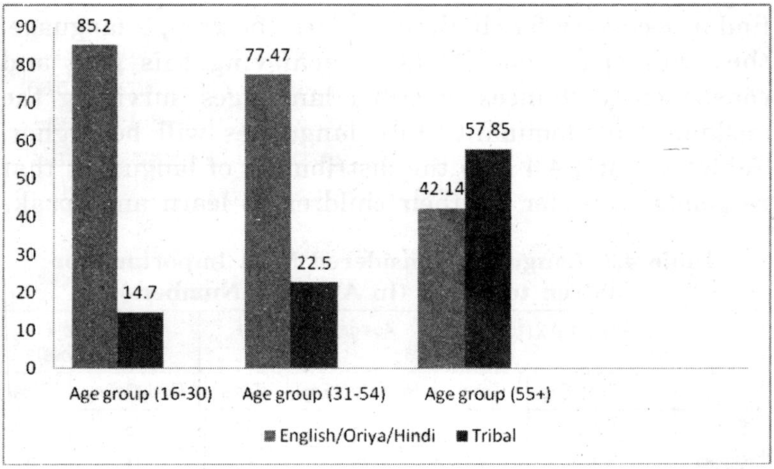

Fig. 4.2: Language Considered More Important for Children to Learn

the highest rate of non-tribal language preference for children (87 per cent). Positive attitude towards ethnic language, among the remaining age groups, on the other hand, has been observed with increasing degree of significance. Over 77 per cent of the third group and 42.14 per cent of the fourth group wanted their children to speak Hindi/Odia/English. This means that 22.5 per cent of the third group and 57.85 per cent of the fourth group supported local vernacular maintenance for ideological and symbolic reasons. The figure for the fourth group is obvious as older generation of the people is very much concerned about the continuity of their language. This tendency was registered by 16 per cent of the sample distributed as follows: 75 per cent of the Sadri, 80 per cent of the Munda group, 78.2 per cent of the Kudukh group, 75 per cent of the Khadia, and 71.42 per cent of the Kisan.

In contrast, 22.5 per cent of the third group supported maintenance of their languages by indicating the necessity of mastering vernaculars on the part of their children. This claim was found among 12 informants of the Sadri

(29.2 per cent), 11 informants of the Munda group (26.8 per cent), 9 informants of the Kudukh group (21.95 per cent), 4 informants of the Khadia (9.7 per cent), and 5 informants of the Kisan (12 per cent). A significant difference is seen in the language preference of adults, across groups, for their children to speak. The younger adults or parents are more concerned for their children to learn the dominant languages of the state as compared to the older parents who are more concerned with the continuity of their mother-tongues. During personal interaction, it was seen that all the groups were unanimous in their need for ethnic language continuity among the next generation. They tend to identify with their language as an effective mechanism of maintaining their ethnic traditions. Yet, as pointed earlier in the qualitative analysis, it is more at the ideological level than anything else. Real efforts are lacking at all levels.

Language Choice with Regard to Domains

In this section of our analysis of language attitude, we are going to investigate the reasons behind preference for a certain language by the population under study. Tables 4.5 and 4.6 give the reasons for language preference according to age.

Table 4.5: Domains Determining Language Choice (in Numbers)

	Age group 1 (5-15)		*Age group 2 (16-30)*		*Age group 3 (31-54)*		*Age group 4 (55 and above)*	
	Hindi/Or/ Eng	*Tribal*	*Hin/ Or/Eng*	*Tribal*	*Hin/Or/ Eng*	*Tribal*	*Hin/Or/ Eng*	*Tribal*
Educational	353	2	217	6	175	7	120	20
Social	320	35	200	23	150	32	10	130
Economic	350	5	213	10	171	11	120	20
Religious	25	330	23	200	10	172	0	120
Symbolic	45	310	36	187	27	155	0	120
Educational	353	2	217	6	175	7	120	20

Table 4.6: Domains Determining Language Choice (in Percentage)

	Age group 1 (5-15)		*Age group 2 (16-30)*		*Age group 3 (31-54)*		*Age group 4 (55 and above)*	
	Hindi/Or/ Eng	*Tribal*	*Hin/ Or/Eng*	*Tribal*	*Hin/Or/ Eng*	*Tribal*	*Hin/Or/ Eng*	*Tribal*
Educational	0.56	97.3	2.6	96.15	3.84	85.71	14.28	96.11/ 99.43
Social	90.14	9.86	89.6	10.3	82.41	17.5	7.14	92.85
Economic	98.59	1.4	95.5	4.48	93.95	6.04	85.71	14.28
Religious	7.04	92.95	10.31	89.6	5.49	94.5	0	100
Symbolic	12.6	87.3	16.14	83.8	14.83	85.16	0	100
Educational	0.56	97.3	2.6	96.15	3.84	85.71	14.28	96.11/ 99.43

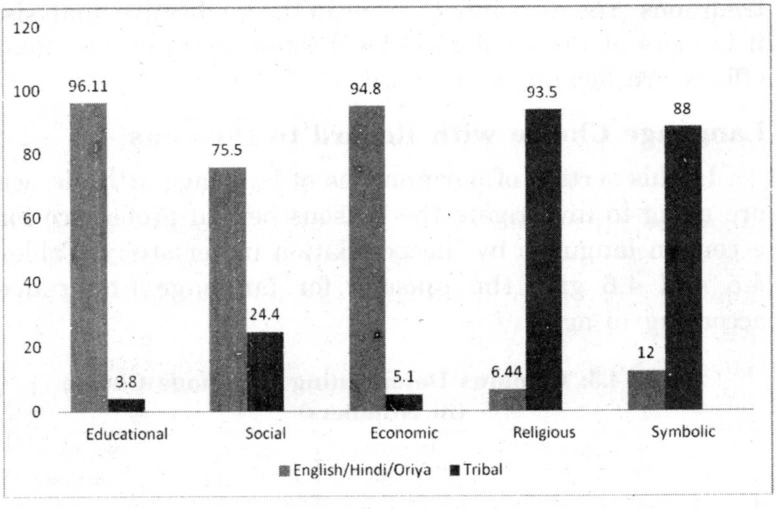

Fig. 4.3: Language Considered more Important with Regard to Domains (all age groups)

Table 4.6 shows that 96.11, 75.5 and 94.8 per cent of all age groups reported that they preferred to speak Hindi/ Odia/English. Preference for these languages was attributed to three components: educational, social and economic. 93.5 and 88 per cent of all age groups preferred the tribal languages for religious and symbolic (symbolising group's ethnic identity) purposes. In other words, English/Hindi/Odia has been classified as an important language on the basis of the greater role it plays in the social, economic and educational aspects of minority groups' everyday life. Ethnic languages, on the other hand, were preferred by 92.95 and 87.3 per cent of the first age group, 89.6 and 83.8 per cent of second age group, 94.5 and 85.16 per cent of the third age group and 100 per cent for fourth age group for religious and symbolic reasons. This is a clear indication that the role of ethnic languages in the life of these tribal communities is relatively limited.

The table also shows that the distribution of the five attitude components towards Hindi/Odia and English differs significantly from the first to the fourth age group. For the first three groups, Hindi/Odia/English was reported by 98.43 per cent for educational reasons, 89.87 per cent for social reasons and 97 per cent for economic reasons. Therefore, we can come to the conclusion that almost 95 per cent of these age groups do not see their ethnic languages as playing practical roles in their daily life.

A very interesting observation to be made from this stratification is that the proportion of Hindi/Odia/English preference increases significantly from the fourth age group to the first one. Over 99.43 per cent of the first, 97.3 per cent of the second and 96.15 per cent of the third group respondents reported that they preferred Hindi/Odia/English because it was the language of education. Furthermore, 90.14 per cent (first), 89.6 per cent (second) and 82.41 per cent (third) preferred Hindi/Odia/English for social interaction and 98.59 per cent (first), 95.5 per cent (second) and 93.95 per cent (third) prefer Hindi/Odia/English for economic reasons. This means that about 93.6 per cent of these groups viewed Hindi/Odia/English as a very important instrument for meeting their everyday life needs. On the other hand, only 3.8, 24.4 and 5.1 per cent of the fourth age group people prefer English/Hindi/Odia for educational, social and economic reasons. This is a clear indication that Hindi/Odia/English constitute the prime concern of the second-generation ethnic minority groups' future plans and perspectives, which negatively influences the status and maintenance of ethnic languages.

Positive attitude towards Hindi/Odia/English among younger generation respondents as shown by Tables 4.5 and 4.6 seems to have three major components. The first of these is educational: "I would like to speak Hindi/Odia/English because these are the languages of education." Such statements were reported by over 97 per cent of the first three group respondents. The second component is social represented by statements such as ("I would like to speak Hindi/Odia/English because it enables me to communicate with others"), ("Hindi/Odia/English is *the* language of communication"), etc. Such statements were reported by 87 per cent of the first three age groups.

The third attitude component is religious in nature: ("I use my mother-tongue to offer my prayers"), ("I would like to speak my mother-tongue because it is the language of my forefathers"), ("The mother-tongue should be spoken because it is the symbol of my tribal heritage") reported by over 92.35 per cent of the three age groups. Preference of mother-tongues for religious purposes is seen more in the third and fourth age groups in comparison to the first two groups. This indicates that young generation respondents are less concerned with religion compared to their old counterparts. Positive attitude towards Hind/Odia/English, on the other hand, was reported by about 93 per cent of the first three groups for educational, social and economic reasons. The existence of such a positive attitude towards Hindi/Odia/English coupled with a relatively negative attitude towards the ethnic languages among young generation members of ethnic minority groups suggests that the groups in question are more prone to language shift.

Reasons for Children Learning Specific Languages

One of the most interesting features of bilingualism/ multilingualism among subjects of this kind of studies is the high level of inconsistency seen between the verbal responses measuring attitude towards local languages and the actual linguistic behaviour of the population. That is, while a considerable number of these people reported they preferred using ethnic languages in all domains of communication, they actually used the dominant languages more than the tribal languages in most of these domains. This tendency can also be reflected by the language they prefer for their children to learn. Tables 4.7 and 4.8 give parental attitudes towards the languages they want their children to learn.

Table 4.7: Language Considered Most Important for Children to Learn with Regard to Domain (In Absolute Numbers)

	Age group 2 (16-30) 223 respondents		*Age group 3 (31-54) 182 respondents*		*Age group 4 (55 and above) 140 respondents*		*Total (Respondents 545)*	
	Hin/Odia/ Eng	*Tribal*	*Hin/Odia/ Eng*	*Tribal*	*Hin/Odia/ Eng*	*Tribal*	*Hin/Odia/ Eng*	*Tribal*
Educational	218	5	170	12	120	20	508	37
Social	184	39	155	27	32	108	371	174
Economic	200	23	164	18	124	16	488	57
Religious	55	168	32	150	140	0	227	318
Symbolic	16	207	23	181	140	0	179	366

Table 4.8: Language Considered Most Important for Children to Learn with Regard to Domain (in Percentage)

	Age group 2 (16-30) 223 respondents		*Age group 3 (31-54) 182 respondents*		*Age group 4 (55 and above) 140 respondents*		*Total (Respondents 545)*	
	Hin/Odia/ Eng	*Tribal*	*Hin/Odia/ Eng*	*Tribal*	*Hin/Odia/ Eng*	*Tribal*	*Hin/Odia/ Eng*	*Tribal*
Educational	97.75	2.24	93.4	6.59	85.71	14.28	93.21	6.78
Social	82.51	17.4	85.16	14.8	22.85	77.14	68.07	31.92
Economic	89.68	10.3	90.1	9.8	88.57	11.42	89.54	10.45
Religious	24.66	75.33	17.58	82.41	100	0	41.65	58.34
Symbolic	7.17	92.8	23.54	76.45	100	0	32.84	67.15

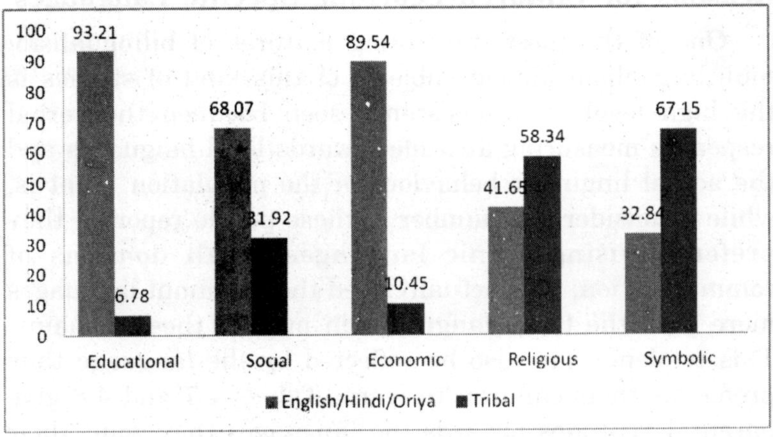

Fig. 4.4: Language Considered More Important for Children to Learn with Regard to Domains (Total, for age groups 2, 3 and 4).

Assessment of Tables 4.7 and 4.8 shows that the first two age group respondents have reported similar attitudes towards the three languages they specified as being very important for their children to learn. Preference of Hindi/ Odia/English was reported by 97.75, 82.51 and 89.68 per cent of the second group, respectively, for the first three domains. All three languages were reported as very important for children by 93.47, 85.16 and 90.1 per cent of the third group, respectively. These figures, when compared with mother tongue retention among the young generation, suggest that the younger parental generation realise the importance of the dominant languages for economic, social and educational purposes and hence wish their children to be thorough with these languages for a better and secure future. Even for the fourth group, a high percentage (85.71 and 88.57 per cent) of people prefers the dominant languages for their children to learn for educational and economic reasons, respectively. For religious and symbolic domains, all the groups reported that they preferred to see their children speak ethnic languages, yet the reality is that a considerable number of the children have already adopted Hindi/Odia/English as the language of communication for almost all purposes. The effect is seen more in township areas, but the village areas are also fast catching up.

Attitudes towards the three languages were found to have more than one component. Among the fourth group respondents, the first factor, education, was reported by 85.71 per cent in favour of Hindi/Odia/English. The second factor, social interaction, was reported by 22.85 per cent in favour of Hindi/Odia/English and the third factor, economic importance, was reported by 88.57 per cent in favour of Hindi/Odia/English. Religion and ethnic traditions, on the other hand, were reported by none in favour of Hindi/Odia/English and 100 per cent in favour of ethnic languages, respectively. The figures suggest that while Hindi/Odia/English was viewed as very important for educational and economic privileges, the importance of vernaculars was limited to religious and ethnic traditions. However, for social interactions, the results reveal a marked difference from the other two groups. Over 78 per cent of the older age group people want their children to interact in their native tongues for intergenerational continuity, but the younger generation is influenced heavily against this by the dominant languages of the area. Since urban life today requires extensive use of Hindi/Odia/English, parents have to accept the fact that their children have to use the language in all domains of communication except at home, where use of ethnic languages is encouraged to emphasise the groups' identity, but that is also getting rapidly influenced by the dominant popular culture and languages of the area.

Among the second and third age groups, language preference for children seems to follow almost the same pattern. Hindi/Odia/English were reported as preferable for educational reasons by 95.57 per cent. The second and third factors 'economic and social communication purposes' were ascribed to Hindi/Odia/English by about 83.83 and

89.8 per cent, respectively. In contrast, the factors, religious and symbolic domains, were ascribed to tribal languages by 78.87 and 84.62 per cent of the second and third group respondents. This indicates that while second and third group parents wished to see their children speaking vernaculars for the sake of maintaining the group's cultural and linguistic heritage, they realise Hindi/Odia/English as very important keys to education, economic interests and for social interactions with non-tribal communities. As a consequence, parents feel that they have to encourage their children to learn the dominant languages at the expense of ethnic languages which apparently have little role to play in their academic and socio-economic life.

The data also indicate that preference of a language in a given domain does not differ significantly across the age groups, except the social domain, which reflects a relatively higher preference for tribal languages for the fourth age group. This can be summed up in a few points. First, we find a more consistent and repeated favouring of Hindi/Odia/English for education among all the generations. This is mainly because people are particularly concerned about securing education for their children. Second, with respect to religion, preference of tribal languages by the old generation is higher than that among young generations. That is, as people advance in age they tend to be more religious than they were during their youth. Third, the greatest degree of preference of Hindi/Odia/English for educational and economic privileges is found among both the young and old generation of people. Since Hindi/Odia/English are always viewed as keys to better job opportunities, it may be logical to assume that it will be the major concern of younger generations. Fourth, old generation respondents slightly surpass their young counterparts in favouring tribal languages, which indicates that tribal language loyalty is stronger among the old generation speakers of ethnic languages.

Correlation between Mother Tongue Maintenance and Language Attitude

In this section, we are going to investigate whether there is a significant relationship between positive attitude towards a language and its mastery as a mother tongue. To this end, the Chi-square test has been employed to process data on subjects' verbal responses about the languages they like best and that they speak natively. This procedure was adopted across the four age groups studied.

In all the four cases, it was found that the estimated Chi-square value was more than the tabulated value (at $c2_{df=20,\ p=0.05}$) of 31.41. That means both the categorical variables are dependent. It was observed that in the last two cases, a larger proportion of respondents speak Odia/Hindi/English, but it is also true that the increase is universal across all language groups.

Fourth Age Group

Tables 4.9 and 4.10 give the relationship between language attitude and mother tongue maintenance among the fourth age group.

Table 4.9: Language Attitude and Mother Tongue Maintenance among the Fourth Age Group (55+ Years, 140 Respondents, in Absolute Numbers)

Mother Tongue Respondents

Preferred Language	*Sadri*	*Munda*	*Kudukh*	*Khadia*	*Kisan*	*Total*
Odia/Hindi/English	8	2	2	1	1	**14**
Sadri	37	10	12	7	8	**74**
Munda		11				**11**
Kudukh			17			**17**
Khadia				12		**12**
Kisan					12	**12**
Total	**45**	**23**	**31**	**20**	**21**	**140**

Table 4.10: Language Attitude and Mother Tongue Maintenance among the Fourth Age Group (55+ Years, 140 Respondents, in Percentage)

Mother Tongue Respondents

Preferred Language	*Sadri*	*Munda*	*Kudukh*	*Khadia*	*Kisan*	*Total*
Odia/Hindi/English	17.7	8.6	6.45	5	4.7	**10**
Sadri	82.2	43.47	38.7	35	38.09	**52.85**
Munda		47.82				**7.85**
Kudukh			54.83			**12.14**
Khadia				60		**8.57**
Kisan					57.14	**8.57**
Total	**32.14**	**16.42**	**22.14**	**14.28**	**15**	**100**

Table 4.10 shows that the two categorical variables are related and a significant relationship exists between language attitude and mother tongue shift among members of the fourth age group. The estimated Chi-square value was found to be c2 = 270.9, which suggests that a significant correlation exists between mastery of a tribal language as a mother tongue and positive attitude towards the language. Moreover, like the rest of the groups, respondents have shown positive attitude towards both Hindi/Odia/English and ethnic language retention. While they reported mastery of ethnic language natively, some of them did prefer to speak Hindi/Odia/English.

The first group respondents displayed a significant association between mastery of tribal languages as a mother tongue and positive attitude towards Hindi/Odia/ English. This suggests that these individuals are consciously aware of the threat to the survival of their own languages. They are, however, unable to do anything about it, given the practical reality of the language situation in Odisha, which tends to favour Hindi/Odia/English rather than the ethnic languages. The speakers of minority languages are unwilling to lose their languages, but they also need to get access to the socio-economic benefits associated with the mastery of Hindi/Odia/English in the country, in general, and in Odisha, in particular.

Third Age Group

Tables 4.11 and 4.12 give the relationship between language attitude and mother tongue maintenance among members of the third age group.

Table 4.11: Language Attitude and Mother Tongue Maintenance among the Third Age Group (31–54 Years, 182 Respondents, in Absolute Numbers)

Mother Tongue Respondents

Preferred Language	*Sadri*	*Munda*	*Kudukh*	*Khadia*	*Kisan*	*Total*
Odia/Hindi/English	32	10	7	5	2	**56**
Sadri	36	17	10	8	4	**75**
Munda		15				**15**
Kudukh			23			**23**
Khadia				8		**8**
Kisan					5	**5**
Total	68	42	40	21	11	182

Table 4.12: Language Attitude and Mother Tongue Maintenance among the Third Age Group (31 – 54 Years, 182 Respondents, in Percentage)

Mother Tongue Respondents

Preferred Language	*Sadri*	*Munda*	*Kudukh*	*Khadia*	*Kisan*	*Total*
Odia/Hindi/English	47.05	23.8	17.5	23.8	18.18	**30.76**
Sadri	52.94	40.47	25	38	36.36	**41.2**
Munda		35.71				**8.24**
Kudukh			37.5			**12.6**
Khadia				38		**4.39**
Kisan					45.45	**2.7**
Total	37.36	23.07	21.9	11.5	6.04	100

Tables 4.11 and 4.12 show that that the two categorical variables are related and a significant relationship is present between mother tongue retention and language preference among members of the third age group. The estimated Chi-square value was found to be c2 = 285.4, which suggests that a significant correlation exists between mastery of a tribal language as a mother tongue and positive attitude towards the language. The degree of association between mastery of ethnic languages as mother tongues and their preference appeared to be especially remarkable among the Sadri group. This confirms our finding that Sadri, till now, is considered to be an important language for the tribals of the area, with most of them viewing it as a symbol of their ethnic identity.

Second Age Group

Tables 4.13 and 4.14 give the relationship between language attitude and mother tongue maintenance among young respondents.

Table 4.13: Language Attitude and Mother Tongue Maintenance among the Second Age Group (16 - 30 Years, 223 Respondents, in Absolute Numbers) Mother Tongue Respondents

Preferred Language	*Sadri*	*Munda*	*Kudukh*	*Khadia*	*Kisan*	*Total*
Odia/Hindi/English	56	20	15	12	13	**116**
Sadri	33	11	8	6	7	**65**
Munda		15				**15**
Kudukh			11			**11**
Khadia				8		**8**
Kisan					8	**8**
Total	89	46	34	26	28	223

Table 4.14: Language Attitude and Mother Tongue Maintenance among the Second Age Group (16–30 Years, 223 Respondents, in Percentage) Mother Tongue Respondents

Preferred Language	*Sadri*	*Munda*	*Kudukh*	*Khadia*	*Kisan*	*Total*
Odia/Hindi/English	62.92	43.4	44.11	46.15	46.42	**52**
Sadri	37.07	23.91	23.52	23.07	25	**29.14**
Munda		32.6				**6.72**
Kudukh			32.35			**4.93**
Khadia				30.7		**3.58**
Kisan					28.57	**3.58**
Total	39.91	20.62	15.24	11.65	12.5	100

Table 4.14 shows that the two categorical variables are related and a significant relationship is present between the language preference and mother-tongue retention among members of the second age group. The estimated Chi-square value was found to be c2 = 241.8, which suggests that a significant correlation exists between mastery of a tribal language as a mother tongue and positive attitude towards the language. This means that ethnic language maintenance and positive attitude towards them go hand in hand among a majority of the vernacular-speaking younger generation surveyed. The table also shows that a contradictory relationship was found between positive attitude towards ethnic languages and their mastery natively among a considerable portion of the younger generation. In other words, a good proportion of young-generation tribals, who spoke their ethnic languages natively (52 per cent), reported that they preferred to speak Hindi/Odia/English. Preference of Hindi/Odia/English in this case is primarily due to the fact that Hindi/Odia/English are essential keys to education, social interaction, and economic success.

First Age Group

Tables 4.15 and 4.16 give the relationship between language attitude and mother tongue maintenance among very young respondents.

Table 4.15: Language Attitude and Mother Tongue Maintenance among the First Age Group 1 (5-15 Years, 355 Respondents, in Absolute Numbers)
Mother Tongue Respondents

Preferred Language	*Sadri*	*Munda*	*Kudukh*	*Khadia*	*Kisan*	*Total*
Odia/Hindi/English	117	22	25	15	15	**194**
Sadri	50	25	26	12	13	**126**
Munda		15				**15**
Kudukh			10			**10**
Khadia				7		**7**
Kisan					3	**3**
Total	167	62	61	34	31	355

Table 4.16: Language Attitude and Mother Tongue Maintenance among the First Age Group 1 (05–15 Years, 355 Respondents, in Percentage)
Mother Tongue Respondents

Preferred Language	*Sadri*	*Munda*	*Kudukh*	*Khadia*	*Kisan*	*Total*
Odia/Hindi/English	70.05	35.48	40.98	44.11	48.38	**54.64**
Sadri	29.94	40.32	42.62	35.29	41.93	**35.49**
Munda		24.19				**4.22**
Kudukh			16.39			**2.11**
Khadia				20.5		**1.97**
Kisan					9.67	**0.84**
Total	47.04	17.46	17.18	9.57	8.7	100

Table 4.16 shows that a significant relationship was present between language preference and mother-tongue

retention among members of the first age group. The estimated Chi- square value was found to be c2 = 234.0, which suggests that a significant correlation exists between mastery of a tribal language as a mother tongue and positive attitude towards the language. A good proportion of young-generation tribals, who spoke their ethnic languages natively (55 per cent), reported that they preferred to speak Hindi/Odia/English. Preference of Hindi/ Odia/English in this case is again primarily because Hindi/ Odia/English are believed to be the essential keys to education, social interactions, and economic successes.

Similar kind of sentiments are shared by most educated tribal natives of the place: Nancy Ekka, an MA student from Rourkela, observes that learning one's mother tongue, which may officially be just a dialect, is not practical any more. "If you have to earn a decent livelihood, you have to learn English or Hindi or whatever is the dominant language of the region. Otherwise you are reduced to labouring in the fields of the dominant classes." L. Toppo, a retired employee of Rourkela Steel Plant and settled in Rourkela, says, "My children studied in Hindi, Odia and English and have settled down in Odisha. Their children speak Hindi as their preferred first language. Though at home, sometimes, we speak Kudukh and Sadri, yet so many words, and with them so many aspects of our mother culture and native tradition, are lost to them. It is a big challenge to save our language in a rapidly globalising world."

Following is the current language situation of the five tribal languages of Sundargarh district of Odisha, as deducted from the information elicited from the respondents:

Current Situation of Sadri Language of Sundargarh District of Odisha

Data was collected from four age groups of people from both the genders as mentioned above (5–15, 16–30, 31–54, 55 and above), and from both the township and village areas. No major differences in opinion could be seen among the male and the female respondents, and only minor differences in opinion were perceived in the responses received from the different age groups. Sadri is more used in the urban areas than in the villages.

- Number of speakers in the region: 2,00,000 (rough estimate).
- No written form/no script of its own. No official status. Sometimes written using Odia script.
- Almost all the people are bilingual or multilingual. Each tribal community has a separate mother tongue like Kudukh, Munda or Khadia. Sadri is the lingua franca of the region, basically in the township areas. Along with Sadri, the people interact in other dominant languages of the region like Odia, Hindi and English with people from non-tribal communities and also with each other. Particularly in the township areas, the educated younger generation communicates in Odia, Hindi or English. The less educated or illiterate young generation also mixes it up with Odia, Hindi and English. The older generation, that is 55 years and above, tries to speak exclusively in Sadri, but is not allowed to do so by the younger generation of people who prefer to mix it up with the major languages of the region. Even then, it is widely used among the people of all the age groups. In the current scenario, it is being seen that Sadri has almost replaced Kudukh, Munda, Khadia and Kisan as the language of communication of the tribal people of the urban areas of Sundargarh district. In the villages, the mother tongues are more widely used within families and at the community level. Sadri is not used very widely.
- Influence of Odia and Hindi is seen to be more as the children get their primary education in these languages. Code-mixing with Odia, Hindi and English

is seen widely among both the adults and the young. But the borrowing is one-sided. Odia and Hindi speakers do not code-mix with Sadri.

- Intergenerational transmission of the language is still happening. But the young age group users are increasingly getting influenced by Odia, Hindi and English.
- The general perception among the tribals is that Odia people, to some extent, are interested to know about their language, but that is probably at a very superficial level. Serious interest in the language is seen to be lacking among the non-tribals.
- Migration to town areas has resulted in people getting their children educated in English, Hindi and Odia medium schools for a better future. Hence, the mother tongue, which is seen to be serving no practical purpose, is facing serious threat from these dominant languages among all the age groups of the people. As a result, number of speakers of the language has decreased over the years.
- The language, sometimes, gets media promotion through cultural shows in local radio and television programmes. But that is very few and far between.
- It does not have a literary tradition. The literature exists only in songs, dance, music and stories that are passed down orally from one generation to the other. Also used orally during religious festivals, marriage ceremonies, etc.
- It is also used to communicate in local business transactions among the various tribal communities.
- Frequency of members of each generation using the language with people of other generations:

Elderly men and women - among each other: *always*
Elderly people with adults: *more in this language than others.*

Elderly people with the young age group: *equally often in either language.*

Elderly people with children: *equally often in either language.*

Adult men with adult men: *equally often in either language.*

Adult women with adult women: *more in this language than others.*

Adults with the young: *equally often in either language.*

Adults with children: *equally often in either language.*

Young with young: *equally often in either language.*

Young with children: *equally often in either language.*

Children among each other: *equally often in either language / sometimes more in other languages than this one.*

- The people across all age groups have responded that they take pride in their language, and are highly concerned about its preservation. But, due to lack of any written materials and books, and primary education being imparted in the state language, the young generation is allowing Odia, Hindi and English to replace their mother-tongue. The parental generation is also not making any effort to pass on the language to their children.
- The people are not aware of any government organisation existing locally for linguistic policy and planning with respect to their language. A few local cultural organisations, sometimes, organise seminars and cultural programmes for promotion of the language. But that is very few and far between.
- Solutions offered by the stakeholders: Government sponsored cultural programmes, seminars and awareness camps could be organised. Own script to

be developed and schools should be equipped with books and materials to teach their language. There should be a compulsion from the government for the natives to be proficient in their mother-tongues if they wished to get into government service. The subject could be taught compulsorily to the children just like it has been made compulsory to teach Odia till a certain level even in English medium schools throughout the state.

- The general tribal feeling is that without government support and persuasion the average tribal would not take the effort to preserve his language, even with all that concern and distress that he experiences with the gradual loss of his language and culture.

Current Situation of Munda Language of Sundargarh District of Odisha

Data was collected from four age groups of people from both the genders as mentioned above (5 – 15, 16 – 30, 31-54, 55 and above), from both the township and village areas. No major differences in opinion could be seen among the male and the female respondents, and only minor differences in opinion were perceived in the responses received from the different age groups. Munda is used more in the village areas than in the towns. The township people rarely use the language even at the inter-community level. For the urban tribals, the lingua franca is Sadri and it is found to be widely used among family and friends too.

- Number of speakers in the region: 1, 64, 765 (as per the 2001 Census).
- No written form/no script of its own. No official status. Almost all the people are bilingual or multilingual. Along with Munda, the people interact in other dominant languages of the region like Sadri, Odia, Hindi and English with the people from non-tribal communities and also with each other. Particularly

in the township areas, the educated younger generation communicates in Sadri, Odia, Hindi or English. The less educated or illiterate young generation also mixes it up with Odia, Hindi and English. The older generation, that is 55 years and above, tries to keep in touch with the language of their ancestors but is not allowed to do so by the younger generation of people who prefer to mix it up with the major languages of the region. Only in the villages, Munda is widely used among the people of all the age groups at the community level. Sadri is not used very widely. Even then, the influence of Odia and Hindi is gradually gathering pace.

- Influence of Odia and Hindi is seen to be more as the children get their primary education in these languages. Code mixing with Odia, Hindi and English is seen widely among both the adults and the young. However, the borrowing is one-sided. Odia and Hindi speakers do not code-mix with Munda.
- Intergenerational transmission of the language is still happening, but only in the village areas. In the township, even the parental generation has lost touch with the language. They do not teach it to their children. In the young generation, very few people are fluent in the language.
- The general perception among the tribals is that non-tribals are completely ignorant about their language. The government is only interested in promoting Odia. They are in no way bothered or concerned about the Munda language. The young age group even perceives that their non-tribal friends look down upon their language.
- Migration to town areas has resulted in people getting their children educated in English, Hindi and Odia medium schools for a better future. Hence, the mother-tongue, which is seen to be serving no practical

purpose, is facing serious threat from these dominant languages among all the age groups of the people. As a result, the number of speakers of the language has decreased over the years.

- It does not have a literary tradition. The literature exists only in songs, dance, music and stories that are passed down orally from one generation to the other. Also used orally during religious festivals, marriage ceremonies, etc., but in urban areas that is also diminishing. Sadri is replacing Munda even during religious ceremonies, local festivities, marriage ceremonies, etc.
- It is rarely used to communicate in local business transactions among the various tribal communities. In towns, Sadri is the lingua franca.
- Frequency of members of each generation using the language with the people of other generations:

In Township Areas

Elderly men and women - among each other: *always*

Elderly people with adults: *more in this language than others.*

Elderly people with the young age group: *equally often in either language.*

Elderly people with children: *equally often in either language.*

Adult men with adult men: *equally often in either language.*

Adult women with adult women: *more in this language than others.*

Adults with the young: *equally often in either language.*

Adults with children: *equally often in either language.*

Young with young: *equally often in either language.*

Young with children: *equally often in either language.*

Children among each other: *equally often in either language / sometimes more in* other languages than this one.

In Village Areas

In village areas, the frequency of members of each generation using the language with people of other generations is quite high, but is decreasing day-by-day with the influence of primary education being imparted in Odia, Hindi and English.

- The people across all age groups have responded that they take pride in their language, and are highly concerned about its preservation. However, due to lack of any written materials and books, and primary education being imparted in the state language, the young generation is allowing Odia, Hindi and English to replace their mother-tongue. The parental generation is also not making any effort to pass on the language to their children. The effect has been such that quite a few Munda language words are almost obsolete now. Munda words such as da?a? (water), sisha? (pencil), adha? (house), layanga (agricultural land), dube?m (to seat), da?ru (tree), hanar (to roam), etc., are no longer being used by the native speakers of the langugae. Instead they use either the Sadri words or the Odia words for these terms in their day to day vocabulary.
- The people are not aware of any government or private organisation existing locally for linguistic policy and planning with respect to this language.
- *Solutions offered by the stakeholders*: Government sponsored cultural programmes, seminars and awareness camps could be organised. Own script to be developed or the Odia script could be used for writing, and schools should be equipped with books

and materials to teach their language. The mass media could also take a more proactive approach in highlighting and promoting the tribal languages of the region. Language centres could also be set up locally with local educated people drafted into the centres to work for the preservation and promotion of the language.

- The general tribal feeling is that without government support and persuasion the average tribal would not take the effort to preserve his language, even with all that concern and distress that he experiences with the gradual loss of his language and culture.

Current Situation of Kudukh (Oraon) Language of Sundargarh District of Odisha

Data was collected from four age groups of people from both the genders as mentioned (5 – 15, 16 – 30, 31–54, 55 and above), from both the township and village areas. No major differences in opinion could be seen among the male and the female respondents, and only minor differences in opinion were perceived in the responses received from the different age groups. Kudukh is used more in the village areas than in the towns. The township people rarely use the language even at the inter-community level. For the urban tribals, the lingua franca is Sadri and it is found to be widely used among family and friends too.

- Number of speakers in the region: 2,10,004 (as per the 2001 Census).
- No written form/no script of its own. No official status. Almost all the people are bilingual or multilingual. Along with Kudukh, the people interact in other dominant languages of the region like Sadri, Odia, Hindi and English with people from non-tribal communities and also with each other. Particularly in the township areas, the educated younger generation communicates in Sadri, Odia, Hindi or

English. The less educated or illiterate young generation also mixes it up with Odia, Hindi and English. The older generation, that is 55 years and above, tries to keep in touch with the language of their ancestors but is not allowed to do so by the younger generation of people who prefer to mix it up with the major languages of the region. Only in the villages, Kudukh is widely used among the people of all the age groups at the community level. Sadri is not used very widely. Even then, the influence of Odia and Hindi is gradually gathering pace.

- Influence of Odia and Hindi is seen to be more as the children get their primary education in these languages. Code mixing with Odia, Hindi and English is seen widely among both the adults and the young. The borrowing is one-sided. Odia and Hindi speakers do not code-mix with Kudukh. However, loan words from dominant languages, until now, have not made any words obsolete. Yet major language words like meal, aanda (egg), bhaat (rice), sabji (curry), kichina-hin (nothing), kaana (what), etc., are widely used rather than the original Kudukh words.
- Intergenerational transmission of the language is still happening, but only in the village areas. In the township, even the parental generation has lost touch with the language. They do not teach it to their children. In the young generation, very few people are fluent in the language.
- The general perception among the tribals is that non-tribals are completely ignorant about their language. They are in no way bothered or concerned about the Kudukh language. The young age group even perceives that their non-tribal friends look down upon their language. A few of 5-15 age group respondents had also responded that they were not very proud of their cultural and linguistic heritage and sometimes

identified themselves with the mainstream culture and languages and tried to hide their tribal identity.

- Migration to town areas has resulted in people getting their children educated in English, Hindi and Odia medium schools for a better future. Hence, the mother tongue, which is seen to be serving no practical purpose, is facing serious threat from these dominant languages among all the age groups of people. As a result, numbers of speakers have decreased over the years.
- It does not have a literary tradition. The literature exists only in songs, dance, music and stories that are passed down orally from one generation to the other. Also used orally during religious festivals, marriage ceremonies, etc., but in urban areas that is also diminishing. Sadri is replacing Kudukh even during religious ceremonies, local festivities, marriage ceremonies, etc.
- It is rarely used to communicate in local business transactions among the various tribal communities. In towns, Sadri is the lingua franca.
- Frequency of members of each generation using the language with people of other generations:

In Township Areas

Elderly men and women - among each other: *always*

Elderly people with adults: *more in this language than others.*

Elderly people with the young age group: *equally often in either language.*

Elderly people with children: *equally often in either language.*

Adult men with adult men: *equally often in either language*.

Adult women with adult women: *more in this language than others*.

Adults with the young: *equally often in either language.*

Adults with children: *equally often in either language.*

Young with young: *more in other languages than this one.*

Young with children: *more in other languages than this one.*

Children among each other: *always in other languages than this one.*

In Village Areas

In village areas the frequency of members of each generation using the language with people of other generations is quite high, but is decreasing day-by-day with the influence of primary education being imparted in Odia, Hindi and English.

- Sometimes it is telecast in radio and television dance and music programmes during Karma, Holi, Jyestha Purnima, Diwali festivals, etc.
- The people across all age groups have responded that they take pride in their language, and are highly concerned about its preservation. But, due to lack of any written materials and books, and primary education being imparted in the state language, the young generation is allowing Odia, Hindi and English to replace their mother-tongue. The parental generation is also not making any effort to pass on the language to their children.
- The people are not aware of any government organisation existing locally for linguistic policy and planning with respect to this language. The general tribal perception is that the government is not interested in promotion or preservation of their

language and culture. A few private organisations exist locally, which organise seminars and cultural programmes occasionally.

- *Solutions offered by the stakeholders*: Government sponsored cultural programmes, seminars and awareness camps could be organised. Own script to be developed or the Odia script could be used for writing, and schools should be equipped with books and materials to teach their language. The mass media could also take a more proactive approach in highlighting and promoting the tribal languages of the region. Language centres could also be set up locally with local educated people drafted into the centres to work for the preservation and promotion of the language. The young people feel that the older generation should take more effort in passing on the language to the future generations. The sincerity to preserve the language should be reflected more in action rather than stay limited to paper only.
- The general tribal feeling is that without government support and persuasion, the average tribal would not take the effort to preserve his language, even with all that concern and distress that he experiences with the loss of his language and culture.

Current Situation of Khadia Language of Sundargarh District of Odisha

Data was collected from four age groups of people from both the genders as mentioned (5–15, 16–30, 31–54, 55 and above), from both the township and village areas. No major differences in opinion could be seen among the male and the female respondents, and only minor differences in opinion were perceived in the responses received from the different age groups. Khadia is used more in the village areas than in the towns. The township people rarely use the language even at the inter-community level. For the urban tribals, the lingua franca is Sadri and it is found to be widely used among family and friends too.

- Number of speakers in the region: 1, 05,099 (as per the 2001 Census).
- No written form/no script of its own. No official status. Almost all the people are bilingual or multilingual. Along with Khadia, the people interact in other dominant languages of the region like Sadri, Odia, Hindi and English with people from non-tribal communities and also with each other. Particularly in the township areas, the educated younger generation communicates in Sadri, Odia, Hindi or English. The less educated or illiterate young generation also mixes it up with Odia, Hindi and English. The older generation, that is 55 years and above, tries to keep in touch with the language of their ancestors but is not allowed to do so by the younger generation of people who prefer to mix it up with the major languages of the region. Only in the villages, Khadia is widely used among the people of all the age groups at the community level. Sadri is not used very widely. Even then, the influence of Odia and Hindi is gradually gathering pace.
- Influence of Odia and Hindi is seen to be more as the children get their primary education in these languages. Code mixing with Odia, Hindi and English is seen widely among both the adults and the young. However, the borrowing is one-sided. Odia and Hindi speakers do not code-mix with Khadia.
- Intergenerational transmission of the language is still happening, but only in the village areas. In the urban areas, even the parental generation has lost touch with the language. They do not teach it to their children. In the young generation, very few people are fluent in the language.

- The general perception among the tribals is that non-tribals are completely ignorant about their language. The government is only interested in promoting Odia. They are in no way bothered or concerned about the Khadia language. The young age group even perceives that their non-tribal friends look down upon their language.
- Migration to urban areas has resulted in people getting their children educated in English, Hindi and Odia medium schools for a better future. Hence, the mother tongue, which is seen to be serving no practical purpose, is facing serious threat from these dominant languages among all the age groups of people. As a result, numbers of speakers have decreased over the years.
- It does not have a literary tradition. The literature exists only in songs, dance, music and stories that are passed down orally from one generation to the other. Also used orally during religious festivals, marriage ceremonies, etc., but in urban areas that is also diminishing. Sadri is replacing Khadia even during religious ceremonies, local festivities, marriage ceremonies, etc.
- It is rarely used to communicate in local business transactions among the various tribal communities. In towns, Sadri is the lingua franca.
- Frequency of members of each generation using the language with people of other generations:

In Township Areas

Elderly men and women - among each other: *equally often in either language.*

Elderly people with adults: *equally often in either language.*

Elderly people with the young age group: *more in other languages than this one.*

Elderly people with children: *more in other languages than this one.*

Adult men with adult men: *equally often in either language.*

Adult women with adult women: *equally often in either language.*

Adults with the young: *more in other languages than this one.*

Adults with children: *more in other languages than this one.*

Young with young: *more in other languages than this one.*

Young with children: *more in other languages than this one.*

Children among each other: *always in other languages.*

In Village Areas

In village areas, the frequency of members of each generation using the language with people of other generations is quite high, but it is decreasing day-by-day with the influence of primary education being imparted in Odia, Hindi and English.

- The people across all age groups have responded that they take pride in their language, and are highly concerned about its preservation. However, due to lack of any written materials and books, and primary education being imparted in the state language, the young generation is allowing Odia, Hindi and English to replace their mother-tongue.
- The people are not aware of any government or private organisation existing locally for linguistic policy and planning with respect to this language. A few private organisations exist locally, which organise seminars and cultural programmes occasionally, and even in

these functions very few people participate or show any interest.

- *Solutions offered by the stakeholders*: Government sponsored cultural programmes, seminars and awareness camps could be organised. Own script to be developed or the Odia script could be used for writing, and schools should be equipped with books and materials to teach their language. The mass media could also take a more proactive approach in highlighting and promoting the tribal languages of the region. Language centres could also be set up locally with local educated people drafted into the centres to work for the preservation and promotion of the language.
- The general tribal feeling is that without government support and persuasion, the average tribal would not take the effort to preserve his language, even with all that concern and distress that he experiences with the loss of his language and culture.

Current Situation of Kisan Language of Sundargarh District of Odisha

Data was collected from four age groups of people from both the genders as mentioned (5–15, 16–30, 31–54, 55 and above), from both the township and village areas. No major differences in opinion could be seen among the male and the female respondents, and only minor differences in opinion were perceived in the responses received from the different age groups. Kisan is used more in the village areas than in the towns. The township people rarely use the language even at the inter-community level. For the urban tribals, the lingua franca is Sadri and it is found to be widely used among family and friends too.

- Number of speakers in the region: 1,11,206 (as per 2001 Census).
- No written form/no script of its own. No official status.

Almost all the people are bilingual or multilingual. Along with Kisan, the people interact in other dominant languages of the region like Sadri, Odia, Hindi and English with people from non-tribal communities and also with each other. Particularly in the township areas, the educated younger generation communicates in Sadri, Odia, Hindi or English. The less educated or illiterate young generation also mixes it up with Odia, Hindi and English. The older generation, that is 55 years and above, tries to keep in touch with the language of their forefathers but is not allowed to do so by the younger generation of people who prefer to mix it up with the major languages of the region. Only in the villages, Kisan is widely used among the people of all the age groups at the community level. Sadri is not used very widely. Even then, the influence of Odia and Hindi is gradually gathering pace.

- Influence of Odia and Hindi is seen to be more as the children get their primary education in these languages. Code mixing with Odia, Hindi and English is seen widely among both the adults and the young. But the borrowing is one-sided. Odia and Hindi speakers do not code-mix with Kisan.
- Intergenerational transmission of the language is still happening in the village areas, but Odia is fast replacing it as the children get their elementary education in Odia medium schools. In the township areas, even the parental generation has lost touch with the language. They do not teach it to their children. In the young generation, very few people are fluent in the language.
- The general perception among the tribals is that non-tribals are completely ignorant about their language. The government is only interested in promoting Odia. They are in no way bothered or concerned about the

Kisan language. The young age group even perceives that their non-tribal friends look down upon their language.

- Migration to town areas has resulted in people getting their children educated in English, Hindi and Odia medium schools for a better future. Hence, the mother tongue, which is seen to be serving no practical purpose, is facing serious threat from these dominant languages among all the age groups of people. As a result, numbers of speakers have decreased over the years.
- It does not have a literary tradition. The literature exists only in songs, dance, music and stories that are passed down orally from one generation to the other. Also used orally during religious festivals, marriage ceremonies, etc., but in urban areas that too is diminishing. Sadri is replacing Kisan even during religious ceremonies, local festivities, marriage ceremonies, etc.
- It is rarely used to communicate in local business transactions among the various tribal communities. In towns, Sadri is the lingua franca.
- Frequency of members of each generation using the language with people of other generations:

In Township Areas

Elderly men and women - among each other: *more in this language than others.*

Elderly people with adults: *more in this language than others.*

Elderly people with the young age group: *equally often in either language.*

Elderly people with children: *equally often in either language.*

Adult men with adult men: *equally often in either language.*

Adult women with adult women: *more in this language than others.*

Adults with the young: *equally often in either language.*

Adults with children: *equally often in either language.*

Young with young: *equally often in either language.*

Young with children: *equally often in either language.*

Children among each other: *always in other languages.*

In Village Areas

In village areas the frequency of members of each generation using the language with people of other generations is quite high, but it is decreasing day-by-day with the influence of primary education being imparted in Odia, Hindi and English.

- The people across all age groups have responded that they take pride in their language, and are highly concerned about its preservation. However, due to lack of any written materials and books, and primary education being imparted in the state language, the young generation is allowing Odia, Hindi and English to replace their mother-tongue. The parental generation is also not making any effort to pass on the language to their children.
- The people are not aware of any government or private organisation existing locally for linguistic policy and planning with respect to this language. The general tribal perception is that the government is not interested in promotion or preservation of their language and culture. A few private organisations exist locally, which organise seminars and cultural programmes occasionally, and even in these functions very few people participate or show any interest.
- *Solutions offered by the stakeholders*: Government sponsored cultural programmes, seminars and

awareness camps could be organised. Own script to be developed or the Odia script could be used for writing, and schools should be equipped with books and materials to teach their language. The mass media could also take a more proactive approach in highlighting and promoting the tribal languages of the region. Language centres could also be set up locally with local educated people drafted into the centres to work for the preservation and promotion of the language.

- The general tribal feeling is that without government support and persuasion the average tribal would not take the effort to preserve his language, even with all that concern and distress that he experiences with the loss of his language and culture.

To summarise, we can say that as per the analysis done, centred on the major evaluative factors of language vitality suggested in the document titled *Language Vitality and Endangerment* by the UNESCO Ad Hoc Expert Group on Endangered Languages mentioned above, following is the status of the tribal languages of the Sundargarh district of Odisha:

- *Sadri: Unsafe (Grade–4):* The language is used by some children in all domains; it is used by all children in limited domains.
- *Munda: Definitely endangered (Grade–3):* The language is used mostly by the parental generation and up.
- *Kudukh: Definitely endangered (Grade–3):* The language is used mostly by the parental generation and up.
- *Khadia: Definitely endangered (Grade–3):* The language is used mostly by the parental generation and up.

- *Kisan: Definitely endangered (Grade–3):* The language is used mostly by the parental generation and up.

Case Study Reports

- **Anita Prabha Ekka** (Tribe: Oraon, Sex: Female, Age: 50, Profession: Housewife, Marital Status: Widow, Educational Qualification: Secondary School Pass, Home Location: Rourkela Town, Number of Children: 3, aged 27, 25 and 19, all are highly educated):
- *Languages known:* Oraon, Hindi, Odia, and Sadri.
- Languages known by her three children: Hindi, Odia, Sadri and English.
- Languages used at home with children: Hindi and Odia.
- Languages used by her three children among each other: Hindi.
- Languages used by her three children with their relatives, across any age group: Hindi and Odia.
- Languages used with parents, parents-in-law, relatives and friends of her own age group from both the town and village areas: Oraon, Sadri and sometimes Sundargarhi dialect, Odia and Hindi also.
- Languages used with children of friends and relatives: Odia, Hindi and Sadri.
- Languages used with neighbours from her own age group, who are from Oraon tribe: Oraon.
- Language used with other neighbours: Sadri, Odia and Hindi.
- Languages used with the children and the young people of the neighbourhood: Sadri, Hindi and Odia.
- **Meena Hasda** (Tribe: Munda, Sex: Female, Age: 26, Profession: Nursing, Marital Status: Single, Educational Qualification: Diploma in Nursing from Bhubaneswar, Home Location: Rourkela Town,

Currently working at *Rajasthan Seva Sadan*, Rourkela as a Nurse, Other members in the family: Parents, two sisters and one brother).

- Languages known: Munda, Hindi, Odia, and Sadri.
- Languages used at home with parents: Munda and Odia.
- Languages used among the siblings: Sadri and Odia.
- Languages used by the children with their grandparents and other relatives who reside in Badgaon village of Sundargarh district: Munda.
- Languages used with friends, colleagues and neighbours: Odia, Hindi and Sadri.
- **Pushpa Dungdung** (Tribe: Khadia, Sex: Female, Age: 30, Profession: Housewife, Marital Status: Married, Educational Qualification: High School, Home Location: Rourkela Town, Other Members in the Family: Husband and one son, aged 5 years).
- Languages known: Khadia, Hindi, Odia, and Sadri.
- Languages used at home with husband and son: Khadia and Odia.
- Languages used with relatives: Khadia.
- Languages used with friends: Sadri and Odia.
- Language used with neighbours: Sadri, Odia and Hindi.
- Languages known to her son: Khadia, Sadri, Hindi and Odia.
- Languages used by her son with his friends: Sadri, Hindi and Odia.
- Languages used by her son with their relatives: Khadia.
- **S.K. Lakra** (Tribe: Kisan, Sex: Male, Age: 25, Profession: Government Employee, Marital Status: Single, Educational Qualification: MBA, Home

Location: Rajgangpur town of Sundargarh district, Other Members in the Family: Parents and One Brother).

- Languages known: Hindi, Odia, English and Sadri.
- Languages used at home with parents and brother: Odia and Sadri.
- Languages used with relatives: Odia and Sadri.
- Languages used with friends: Hindi, Sadri and Odia.
- Language used with colleagues and neighbours: Sadri, Odia, Hindi and sometimes English.
- **Sylsvester Dung Dung** (Tribe: Khadia, Sex: Male, Age: 38, Profession: Farmer, Marital Status: Married, Educational Qualification: 7th Standard Pass, Home Location: Jaidega Village, Naotoli Block, Sundargarh District, Other Members in the Family: Wife, one Daughter and two Sons).
- Languages known: Sadri and Khadia.
- Languages known to wife: Sadri, Khadia and a bit of Hindi as she is from Jharkhand.
- Languages known to children: Sadri, Khadia and Odia, as they have started going to the Aganwadi centre in the village, they have picked up Odia from there.
- Languages used at home with wife and children: Sadri and Khadia.
- Languages used with friends, relatives and neighbours: Khadia.
- Language used at the marketplace: Sadri and Khadia
- **Malhar Kindo** (Tribe: Oraon, Sex: Male, Age: 56, Profession: Farmer, Marital Status: Married, Educational Qualification: Primary School, Home Location: Sonakhan Village, near Rajgangpur Town of Sundargarh District, Other Members in the Family: Wife, one Daughter (age, 23) and one Son (age, 19).

- Languages known: Oraon, Sadri Hindi and Odia.
- Languages known to children: Sadri, Hindi, Odia and English.
- Languages used at home with wife and children: Odia and Sundargarhi dialect.
- Languages used with relatives and friends in the neighbourhood: Sadri.
- Languages used with relatives of his own age group, during festivals and other ceremonies: Oraon.
- Languages used with relatives of the next generation, during festivals and other ceremonies: Sadri.
- Language used at the marketplace: Sadri and Odia.
- **D. Ekka** (Tribe: Oraon, Sex: Male, Age: 45, Profession: Farmer, Marital Status: Married, Educational Qualification: Secondary School, Home Location: Kusumdegi Village, Baartoli Block, Sundargarh District, Other Members in the Family: Wife).
- Languages known: Oraon, Sadri, Hindi and Odia.
- Languages used at home with wife: Sadri and Oraon.
- Languages used with relatives and friends in the village: Oraon and Sadri.
- Language used at the marketplace and with people from other villages: Sadri, Hindi and Odia.
- Languages used with relatives and friends from township areas: Oraon, Sadri, Odia and Hindi.
- **Stylene Kerketta** (Tribe: Munda, Sex: Male, Age: 22, Profession: Sweeper, Marital Status: Single, Educational Qualification: Primary School, Home Location: Rourkela Town of Sundargarh District, Other Members in the Family: Parents, two Brothers and two Sisters).
- Languages known: Munda, Sadri, Hindi and Odia.

- Languages used at home with parents: Munda and Sadri.
- Language used among siblings: Sadri.
- Languages used with relatives: Munda and Sadri.
- Languages used with friends: Sadri, Hindi and Odia.
- Language used with colleagues and neighbours: Sadri, Odia and Hindi.

Concluding Remarks

From the above results, it is obvious that the said four tribal languages, Kisan, Munda, Oraon and Khadia, are on the path of decline as intergenerational transmission of these languages is rare. Even if some parents are taking care to transmit the knowledge of the languages to the next generation, once the children are exposed to the Odia/English medium educational system, their language usage priority also starts to change. Their exposure to a perceived superior culture has influenced them enough to adapt the so-called superior languages for a better and secure future. Only Sadri language has been able to sustain its importance until now, in spite of constant pressure from dominant languages like English, Odia and Hindi. The main reasons for this could be the fact that Sadri is the inter-tribal lingua franca on this part of the country and, therefore, a sizable proportion of population of the tribals use it as their everyday language. It acts as a cornerstone of their tribal identity and hence its significance until now. Even then, it remains to be seen how long the language is able to sustain itself under the onslaught of dominant languages of the place like Hindi, English and Odia. As seen from the language status gradation table, Sadri is levelled as 'unsafe', and something that is unsafe implies that it does not have a secure future.

5

Conclusion and Recommendations

In this chapter, based on the results and discussions, the conclusions have been drawn and recommendations given at the end. The study was initially conceived with three basic objectives in mind:

- How far English language and dominant state languages have influenced the tribal languages of north-west Odisha, with special focus on the once dominant languages of Sundargarh district like Munda, Khadia, Kudukh (Oraon), Kisan and Sadri.
- Are these tribal languages on a path of decline, and what does the future hold for such tribal languages of India?
- Why people from subordinate cultures and languages do not make enough effort or adequate measures to preserve their culture and language?

The information elicited from the local tribals of the district yielded certain results that have helped in finding answers to the objectives of the present study.

Conclusions

The study focused on language preference among the

respondents, reasons for language preference, parents' preference of language for their children to speak and the relation between speaking a language natively and attitude towards it. The findings of the study indicate that while younger generations preferred Hindi/Odia/English, their older counterparts showed more concern for indigenous languages. However, both the generations agreed that they preferred Hindi/Odia/English for educational, economic and social reasons and ethnic languages for religious and symbolic issues. Parental attitudes, on the other hand, revealed that tribal groups, across the rural-urban divide, wanted their children to learn Hindi/Odia/English for practical reasons (educational, economic and social) and ethnic languages for religious and symbolic ones (maintaining the group's ethnic identity). A general discrepancy between positive attitude towards ethnic languages and their actual maintenance was also found among a vast majority of the community surveyed, especially the younger generations.

The researcher drew the following conclusions from the findings of the study and theoretical propositions of the related literature:

- Due to industrialisation, urbanisation and economic development of the area, the traditional *Adivasi* institution is almost on the verge of breakdown. This has not only taken its toll on the languages of the *Adivasis,* but also on their entire culture and their way of living. There is a tendency to undervalue and disrespect the rituals and traditions that carried different meanings during the past.
- The customs and practices that once united villages and communities together have started being diluted and do not carry the same significance anymore. The young generation has even started adapting to non-*Adivasi* culture and the way of living which has put the older generation in perpetual anguish but for

which they are unable to offer any solution. This is an aftermath which is seen in every culture-contact situation, so it is hardly surprising that the young tribals are preferring to practise the ways of dominant cultures.

- The older generation understands that their culture, of which language is a subset, is on the verge of extinction. Yet, at the same time, they realise that by holding onto a primitive way of life and living, they would be depriving their younger generation of all the advantages that a modern and a dominant culture brings along with it for the economic upliftment of future generations.
- Ironically, even though the *Adivasis*, across all ages, took pride in their own languages, yet, at the same time, the younger generation is deliberately allowing their tribal languages to perish steadily by refraining from using the language in their speech. A general lack of intergenerational transmission of mother tongues is taking a heavy toll on the local *Adivasi* languages of the area. In village areas, even though intergenerational transmission of mother-tongues is still happening, yet once children start going to schools and colleges, they get highly influenced by the languages of their educational system which are mainly Odia, Hindi and English.
- Sadri still plays a cementing role among the tribal communities in the township areas by virtue of its being the lingua franca. However, the younger generation of the relatively better-off and educated *Adivasis* of the area uses Odia and Hindi languages more than any other language, among themselves. Sadri and other local dialects of their tribes are gradually losing out, and in such a scenario, it is not so difficult to predict the future of these languages.

- The older generation is quite blasé about it and rarely there is any objection to it. The general tendency today is to adapt any language that is aiding towards the economic upliftment of the populace.
- Interestingly, while hundred per cent of the respondents replied in the positive regarding preservation of their tribal languages, the users themselves are seldom taking any measures to preserve them. The will to preserve their languages remains only on the paper. Even though some parents communicate with their children in their ancestral languages, yet once the children start going to schools the influence of Odia or English medium schooling forces them to give more importance to these dominant languages and not their mother-tongues.
- A few extreme cases have also been noted where people have changed their surnames to hide their immediate tribal identities. This is being mainly done by tribals working in government and non-government organisations, as they wish to hide their tribal identity from other tribals in the organisation and from the general caste people. They wish to be largely seen as someone from the general caste, as they feel that their tribal identity might make general caste people to look down upon them. However, ironically, they have not forsaken the reservation benefits that come with their tribal identity.
- Personal interaction with the older generation of *Adivasis* also elicited the fact that *Adivasi* languages were once 'pure languages'. These were pure languages in the sense that, traditionally tribals never made use of abusive words or phrases in their interaction with other tribals. Their needs were simple and they were a simple race without greed, jealousy or hatred being a part of their lifestyle. According to these elderly folks, once their race got assimilated

into the mainstream culture, abusive terms got absorbed into their languages subsequently from dominant languages and cultures of the place.

- It is now a situation where young people have almost started hating their own culture, own language, with the pre-conceived notion that this is what that is keeping them economically and socially backward. Just like their counterparts from other cultures, they also wish to be seen as someone who is cool and smart, and in tune with the times. They perceive their tribal identity to be a barrier in their quest for this assimilation into a mainstream life and lifestyle.
- In the villages, people still use their ancestral languages. Even then, government intervention and promotion is highly essential so that people who migrate to urban areas feel a sense of pride for their language and make special efforts to teach it to the future generation.
- The tribal people feel that the solution to most of their problems lies in the hands of the government. The majority opinion is that the government is not doing enough for them, and lack of proper accountability of the government from its own officials is allowing most beneficial programmes to lose momentum and ultimately result in their failure.

Recommendations

On the basis of the research findings, the author recommends the following to researchers, scholars, linguists, administrators and policy makers. The authorities, applying an inclusive policy where all the stakeholders get adequate opportunity for promotion and preservation of endangered languages, could implement some of the following strategies:

1. ***Providing basic linguistic and pedagogical training***: Adequate training should be provided to

language teachers on language teaching methods and techniques, curriculum development, and teaching materials development. Orientation training for the textbook writers at the first stage and the primary school teachers at the second stage is highly essential. The help of tribal people from different linguistic groups must be taken for this. This training should be both rigorous and quick and should be planned as workshops, at the end of which the trainees would be required to produce textbooks in different tribal languages.

2. ***Supporting and developing the national language policy:*** The Constitution of India makes provision for "... free and compulsory education for all children until they complete the age of fourteen years." But the Constitution has no explicit statements regarding the language(s) to be taught in education or the language(s) through which education has to be imparted. In 1956, the All India Council for Education recommended the adoption of the three-language formula and it was accepted widely and adopted by many states. This three-language policy was reiterated by the National Policy on Education in 1968, yet again in 1986, and was adopted as a Programme of Action by parliament in 1992. Yet, an official review of the three-language formula in the National Curriculum Framework for School Education in January 2000 found that "in a number of states/organisations/ boards, however, the spirit of the formula has not been followed and the mother tongue of the people has been denied the status of the first language ...." Therefore, more social scientists and humanists, and speakers of endangered languages themselves should be actively involved in the formulation of national language policies. In the educational sector, a number of linguists are engaged in implementing increasingly

popular mother tongue education programmes. "So-called mother tongue education, however, often does not refer to education in the ancestral languages of ethno-linguistic minorities (i.e., endangered languages), but rather to the teaching of these languages as school subjects. The most common educational model for teaching ethno-linguistic minority children in schools still uses locally or nationally dominant languages as media of instruction" (UNESCO Ad hoc Expert Group Document on Endangered Languages, 2003). Teaching exclusively in dominant languages supports their spread, but at the expense of endangered languages, which the authorities should try to avoid at the very least.

3. ***Providing training in literacy and local documentation skills:*** Training local language workers to develop orthographies, if needed, read, write, and analyse their own languages, and produce adequate teaching materials. One of the effective strategies here is the establishment of local research/ language centres, where speakers of endangered languages could be trained to study, document and archive their own language materials.

4. ***Proper documentation of the endangered languages:*** A language that can no longer be sustained or revived still deserves to be completely documented. This is because each language encompasses unique cultural and ecological knowledge within it. It is also because languages are diverse and different. "Documentation of such a language is important for several reasons: (1) it enriches the human intellectual property, (2) it presents a cultural perspective that may be new to our current knowledge, and (3) the process of documentation often helps the language resource person re-activate the linguistic

and cultural knowledge" (UNESCO Adhoc Expert Group Document on Endangered Languages, 2003).

5. ***Improving living conditions and respect for the human rights of speaker communities:*** Language documenters, though not directly involved in economic and social development, can help governments identify ignored populations. Linguists and educators can be vital mediators by supporting the communities in formulating claims about their linguistic and other human rights. Conversely, materials such as those on health care, community development, or language education produced for these marginalised communities require specialist input. Concepts and contents need to be conveyed in a culturally meaningful way for complete understanding by the people concerned.

6. ***Selecting proper criteria for deciding upon suitable tribal languages for primary education:*** A committee of experts, sponsored by the UNESCO in 1951 on the use of vernacular languages in education, has reported that a lingua franca is not an adequate substitute for the mother-tongue, unless the children learn the regional languages before coming to the school in the areas where most of the tribals are bilingual. A recent investigation, conducted by the Tribal Research Bureau, Odisha, has revealed that the children in most areas have little or no acquaintance with the Odia language before coming to school. Therefore, there should be proper criteria for fixing up priorities for selecting tribal languages for primary education.

7. ***Potential student population for each linguistic group could be taken as a point of reference:*** The potential student population for each linguistic group should be considered before deciding on imparting primary education to tribal children in their mother-

tongues. No programme of education will be feasible unless there is sufficient number of students. Generally, the area of operation of a primary school is very small, and among the tribes, this area is further limited by geographical factors and social isolation. The area that would serve as a unit for primary education should therefore be determined and its minimum student potentiality based on the individual tribal languages should be assessed. Tentatively, it may be suggested that for the time being a total number of hundred potential primary students within a radius of five kilometres should be accepted as the unit and if ten such units can be located for a linguistic group it would have a claim for primary education in its own language. On this basis, such problems as preparation of textbooks and training of teachers can also be determined.

8. ***Appropriate contents of textbooks***: While preparing the textbooks, due cognizance should be taken of the social and physical environment of specific tribal areas. The culture, the surroundings and the local activities, which the children of different tribes are familiar with, should be carefully enumerated and graded in order of complexity to provide the materials for textbooks for different age groups. This enumeration can be undertaken by the co-operative efforts of anthropologists, linguists, educationists and local tribal people.

9. ***Proper evaluation***: The programme of primary education in tribal language being a new venture, a thorough evaluation after the primary stage and periodical evaluations afterwards would be required to determine its effectiveness. The evaluation of the programme should lay emphasis on the following points:

- How far the programme has been effective in

attracting progressively large number of students towards primary education.

- How far the students receiving primary education in tribal languages are equipped for further education and to what extent they are able to compete with students from other economic and cultural background.

10. ***Ensuring accountability from all the appointed officials:*** Last but not least, the strategies could be made for the authorities to ensure that officials engaged in implementing all on-going tribal languages development programmes and plans are made accountable for their actions so that some measure of success could be derived from all those policies and plans. Otherwise, the strategies would remain only on paper, and the reality would be something vastly different.

Concluding Remarks

According to Crystal (2000), bottom-up initiatives are a top priority, for they help form the ground swell of public opinion that can make governments act. In many parts of the world, 'vociferous activism' on behalf of minority languages is absent or suppressed. Sundargarh is one such example. One of their solutions to their various problems is that government officers, NGO workers, priests, missionaries, etc., should be conversant in their languages, so that they are able to derive the maximum benefits from all the schemes that government and other organisations have reserved for them. However, these officials and volunteers, who come from all over India and from abroad, sometimes take the help of local bilingual people to get their message across and do not normally bother to understand the tribal language.

Mostly, it is seen that a state of *laissez-faire* prevails among the people of the region. To counter this, maybe, a tribal people's movement, which compels the government to make them a part of the decision-making process in reality, and not just as eyewash, has become the need of the hour. Unless there is widespread awareness among the *Adivasis* themselves and the will power to hold on to their culture and language, no amount of government intervention can help these people. At present at Tiklipada village, in Badgaon block of Sundargarh district, all people speak the local Munda language. It is alive and thriving, but for how long, nobody knows.

A universally accepted principle that hardly needs any elaboration is that children should be taught in their mother tongues, especially at the primary level. Indian constitutional position, as far as the tribal people are concerned in this respect, is very clear. Article 4 of the Constitution states this in very clear-cut terms in the following words: "This state shall promote with special care the educational and economic interests of the weaker section of the people, and in particular of the scheduled castes and scheduled tribes, and shall protect them from social injustice and all forms of exploitation."

In addition to this, Article 29 of the Constitution makes a direct reference to language. According to the provisions of this Article, the tribal people are eligible for protection, as cultural minorities, for the conservation of their language, script and culture. This point has been further stressed by the Scheduled Areas and Scheduled Tribe Commission, which while discussing the functions of Tribal Research Institutes located throughout India, has laid special emphasis on "research in tribal philology with a view to prepare textbooks and primes, in tribal languages, collection of folk songs, folk-lore, stories of tribal heroes, etc." Thus as far as constitutional provisions and state policies are concerned, there is a clear-cut mandate for imparting education to the tribal people in their respective languages, especially at the primary stage. It is the implementation part and the technical difficulties associated with the implementation processes that create the problems and lack of interest in achieving the desired targets.

Every day, the world faces new challenges in keeping its languages living and thriving. It is high time the citizens of the world should pool their resources and work collectively on preserving their linguistic and cultural diversity. This requires grouping the resources at all levels; individual language experts, local speaker communities, governmental and institutional organisations, NGOs, etc. At the local community level, no doubt, many people have been working to develop language education programmes, usually with extremely limited technical resources, but unlike teachers of major languages of the world, they not only lack formal training in language teaching, but also the required basic language descriptions. These language teachers require a variety of skills: some are educational in nature (e.g., curriculum and materials development, language teaching techniques and methods); some are sociolinguistic (e.g., analysis of on-going language contact processes, of past and present ancestral language functions); and some are basic linguistic functions (e.g., data collection, analysis and description, etc.).

Similarly, linguists, language activists, and policy makers have a long-term task of compiling and disseminating the most effective and practical mechanisms for sustaining and revitalising the endangered tribal languages of our country. Some other important ways to preserve Indian tribal languages could be like preference for primary education in the mother tongue, promotion of translations and, most importantly, the need for studying the relation between language, society, and politics, something traditional linguists have been wary of doing.

The multitude and diversity of tribal languages in Odisha has not usually been thought of as a resource (Zide 1997). It may be administratively simpler to adapt to the language of the state or the place, but allowing already vulnerable communities to abandon their mother-tongue or their ancestral language deprives the speakers more than they can ever be compensated for. Therefore, probably at some level or the other, we all share the responsibility of ensuring that no language disappears and that all languages are preserved and perpetuated into the future generations. It is a well-known fact that a language never dies; death is imposed upon it, often by external forces, like in the case of India's many *Adivasi* languages. When a language dies, a culture, a way of life dies with it. Hence, it is important to preserve all these languages, as it would be a definite step towards preserving India's cultural and linguistic diversity.

Appendix I

Impact of English and Major Indian Languages on the Tribal Languages of Western Orissa

ପଶ୍ଚିମ ଓଡିଶା ଆଦିବାସୀ ଭାଷାଗୁଡିକ ଉପରେ ଇଂରାଜୀ ଓ ପ୍ରଧାନ ଭାରତୀୟ ଭାଷାମାନଙ୍କ ପ୍ରଭାବ

Sponsored Research Project funded by the Indian Council of Social Science Research (ICSSR), JNU Institutional Area, Aruna Asaf Ali Marg, New Delhi. ଇଣ୍ଡିଆନ କାଉନସିଲ ଅଫ ସୋସିଆଲ ସାଇନ୍ସ ରିସର୍ଚ୍ଚ (ICSSR) ଜେଏନଇଉ ଇନଷ୍ଟିଚ୍ୟୁସନାଲ ଏରିଆ, ଅରୁଣା ଆସଫ ଅଲ୍ଲୀ ମାର୍ଗ, ନିଉ ଡେଲ୍ଲି ଦ୍ୱାରା ଆର୍ଥିକ ଅନୁଦାନ ପ୍ରାପ୍ତ ପ୍ରଣୋଦିତ ଗବେଷଣା ପକଳ୍ପ।

Principal Investigator: Dr. Seemita Mohanty, Associate Professor, Department of Humanities and Social Sciences, National Institute of Technology, Rourkela – 769008 (Orissa).

SURVEY QUESTIONNAIRE ସର୍ବେକ୍ଷଣ (ସର୍ଭେ) ପ୍ରଶ୍ନାବଳୀ

Date of data collection: ତଥ୍ୟ ସଂଗ୍ରହର ତାରିଖ :

Respondent's Details ଉତ୍ତରଦାତାଙ୍କ ପରିଚୟ :

- Sex: ପୁରୁଷ / ମହିଳା :
- Age group: ବୟସ :
  5 - 15   16 - 30   31 - 54   55 and above
  ୫–୧୫   ୧୬–୩୦   ୩୧–୫୪   ୫୫ ରୁ ଅଧିକ

- Location : ସ୍ଥାନର ନାମ :
- Educational background : ଶିକ୍ଷାଗତ ଯୋଗ୍ୟତା :
- Professional background : ଚାକିରିଗତ ଯୋଗ୍ୟତା :
- Financial situation : ଆର୍ଥିକ ଅବସ୍ଥା :

  Comfortable Adequate Inadequate Very Poor

  ସ୍ୱଚ୍ଛଳ ଯଥେଷ୍ଟ ସ୍ୱଚ୍ଛଳ ଅସ୍ୱ ଳ ଅଭାବଗ୍ରସ୍ଥ

Details of Language ଭାଷାଗତ ସୂଚନା :

- Name of language on which data is provided: ସଂଗ୍ରହ କରାଯାଉଥିବା ତଥ୍ୟର ଭାଷା

  Name given to the language by native speakers: ସ୍ଥାନୀୟ ବାସିନ୍ଦାମାନେ ଭାଷାକୁ କେଉଁ ନାମରେ ଜାଣନ୍ତି?

  Name given by the non-native community to the language: ସ୍ଥାନୀୟ ଅଣଭାଷୀ ଗୋଷ୍ଠୀଙ୍କ ଦ୍ୱାରା ଦିଆଯାଇଥିବା ଭାଷାର ନାମ
- What language group does the language belong to? କେଉଁ ଭାଷାଗୋଷ୍ଠିର ଅନ୍ତର୍ଗତ
- Family: ଭାଷା ପରିବାର :
- Group: ଭାଷାଗୋଷ୍ଠୀ : Subgroup: ଉପଗୋଷ୍ଠୀ :
- *(Ref*ସୂଚନା*)*
- **Does this language exist in a written form?** ଏହା ଏକ ଲିଖିତ ଭାଷା କି ?
- **Why do you consider yourself a member of this linguistic community?** ଆପଣ ନିଜକୁ ଏହି ଭାଷାଗୋଷ୍ଠୀର ବ୍ୟକ୍ତି ବୋଲି ଭାବନ୍ତି କି ?
- **What is the total number of inhabitants (whether or not they speak this language) of your community?** (Please give a rough estimate). ଏହି ଭାଷାଗୋଷ୍ଠୀର ଜନସଂଖ୍ୟା କେତେ (ସେମାନେ ଏହି ଭାଷାରେ କଥାବାର୍ତ୍ତା କରନ୍ତି କି) ? (ଏକ ଆନୁମାନିକ ହିସାବ ଦିଅନ୍ତୁ)
- **How many of the inhabitants of your community understand, speak, read or write**

this language? ଆପଣଙ୍କ ଭାଷାଗୋଷ୍ଠୀର କେତେଜଣ ବାସିନ୍ଦା ଭାଷାକୁ ବୁଝିପାରନ୍ତି / କହିପାରନ୍ତି / ଲେଖିପାରନ୍ତି ? (ଚିହ୍ନ ଦିଅନ୍ତୁ)

All	Many	Some	Few
ସମସ୍ତେ	ଅଧିକାଂଶ	କେତେଜଣ ମାତ୍ର	ଜ୍ଳକେତେଜଣ ମାତ

- **How many of the speakers are monolingual (use only this language)?** କେତେଜଣ ବସିନ୍ଦା କେବଳ ଏହି ଗୋଟିଏ ମାତ୍ର ଭାଷା କହନ୍ତି ?

Many	Some	Few	None
ଅଧିକାଂଶ	କେତେଜଣ ମାତ୍ର	ଅଳ୍ପକେତେଜଣ ମାତ୍ର	କେହିକହନ୍ତିନାହିଁ

- **How many of the speakers are bilingual/ multilingual (use this and other languages)? What other language(s) do they speak?** କେତେଜଣ ବସିନ୍ଦା ଦ୍ୱିଭାଷି ବା ଦୁଇଟି ଭାଷା କହନ୍ତି / ବହୁଭାଷି ବା ଏହି ଭାଷା ସହିତ ଅନ୍ୟ କେତେଟା ଭାଷା ବି କହିପରନ୍ତି ? ଅନ୍ୟ କି କି ଭାଷା ସେମାନେ କଥାବାର୍ତ୍ତା କରନ୍ତି ?

All	Many	Some	Few
ସମସ୍ତେ	ଅଧିକାଂଶ	କେତେଜଣ ମାତ୍ର	ଅଳ୍ପକେତେଜଣମାତ

- **How fluent are you in this language? Where do you use this language? What are the other languages that you use for communication and with whom and where?** ଏହି ଭାଷା କହିବାକୁ ଆପଣଙ୍କୁ ସହଜ ଲାଗେ କି? କେଉଁ ମାନଙ୍କ ସହିତ ଆପଣ ଏହି ଭାଷାରେ କଥା ହୁଅନ୍ତି ? ଅନ୍ୟ କେଉଁ ଭାଷାରେ ଆପଣ ଅନ୍ୟମାନଙ୍କ ସହିତ କଥାବାର୍ତ୍ତା କରନ୍ତି, କେଉଁ କେଉଁ ସ୍ଥାନରେ ଓ କେଉଁ କେଉଁ ବିଷୟରେ ?
- **Could you please indicate the extent of code-switching/borrowing (from dominant languages like English, Hindi, and Odia etc.) among the speakers?** (Code-switching: using words and phrases from other languages while speaking.) ଅନ୍ୟମାନଙ୍କ ସହିତ କଥାବାର୍ତ୍ତା କାରିବା ସମୟରେ ଆପଣ ଅନ୍ୟ କେଉଁ ଭାଷାର ସାହାଯ୍ୟ ନିଅନ୍ତି, ଯେପରି ଇଂରାଜି / ହିନ୍ଦି / ଓଡିଆ ବିଭିନ୍ନ ବୟସର ଲୋକମାନଙ୍କ ସହିତ କଥା କହିବା ବିଷୟରେ ସୂଚନା ଦିଅନ୍ତୁ। (କୋଡ–ସ୍ୱିଚିଙ୍ଗ : କଥାବାର୍ତ୍ତା ସମୟରେ ଅନ୍ୟ ଭାଷାର ଶବ୍ଦ ବା ଶବ୍ଦାବଳିର ବ୍ୟବହାର କରିବା)

Elderly Men	*Elderly Women*	*Adult Men*	*Adult Women*	*Young Men*	*Young Women*	*Boys*	*Girls*

Specify the frequency: 4 = frequently; **3** = occasionally; **2** = rarely; **1** = never

ଗୁରୁଜନ ସ୍ତରିୟ ପୁରୁଷ	ଗୁରୁଜନ ସ୍ତରିୟ ସ୍ତ୍ରୀଲୋକ	ବୟସ୍କ ପୁରୁଷ	ବୟସ୍କ ସ୍ତ୍ରୀଲୋକ	ଯୁବକ	ଯୁବତି	ବାଳକ	ବାଳିକା

କଥାବାର୍ତ୍ତା କରିବାର ପରିମାଣ : ୪=ଅଧିକାଂଶ ସମୟରେ
୩=ବେଳେବେଳେ ୨=କେବେକେମିତି / ଅଳ୍ପସମୟରେ ୧=ଜମାକହନ୍ତିନାହିଁ

- **Are you aware whether the borrowing is only one-sided (from the dominant languages to the**

minority language) or is it both ways? ଆପଣ ଜାଣନ୍ତି କି ଅନ୍ୟ ପ୍ରାଧାନ ଭାଷାର (ଇଂରାଜି / ହିନ୍ଦି / ଓଡିଆ) ଶବ୍ଦ / ଶବ୍ଦାବଳୀ ସବୁ ଏହି ଭାଷାରେ ବେଶି ବ୍ୟବହାର ହୁଏ ନା ଉଭୟ ଭାଷା ପରସ୍ପରକୁ ପ୍ରଭାବିତ କରନ୍ତି? (ଅର୍ଥାତ ଆପଣଙ୍କ କଥିତ ଭାଷା ଓ ପ୍ରଧାନ ଭାଷା ଉଭୟରେ କେତେକ ଶବ୍ଦ / ଶବ୍ଦାବଳି ସମାନ ଭାବରେ ବ୍ୟବହାର ହୁଏ)

- **Have the loan-words from dominant languages made any words obsolete (out-dated) in your language? (please give examples)** ଅନ୍ୟ ପ୍ରଧାନ ଭାଷାରୁ ଆସିଥିବା କେଉଁ ଶବ୍ଦ ଆପଣଙ୍କ କଥିତ ଭାଷାର କେଉଁ ଶବ୍ଦ / ଶବ୍ଦାବଳି ସ୍ଥାନରେ ବ୍ୟବହାର ହେଉଛି? (ଦୟା କରି ଉଦାହରଣ ଦିଅନ୍ତୁ ।)
- **Has English, Hindi or Odia influenced your way of speaking/writing in any way, even when you are communicating in your own mother tongue?** ଆପଣ ନିଜ ମାତୃଭାଷାରେ କାଥାବାର୍ତ୍ତା କରିବା ସମୟରେ ବା ଲେଖିବା ସମୟରେ ଇଂରାଜି / ହିନ୍ଦି / ଓଡିଆ ଭାଷାର ସାହାଯ୍ୟ ନିଅନ୍ତି କି?
- **How has the number of speakers of this language evolved over time (increased, decreased or remained stable)?** ଆପଣଙ୍କ ମାତୃଭାଷାର ଲୋକ ସଂଖ୍ୟା ସମୟକ୍ରମେ ବୃଦ୍ଧି ପାଇଛନ୍ତି କି? (ବୃଦ୍ଧିପାଇଚନ୍ତି / କମିଯାଇଚନ୍ତି / ସମାନ ରହିଛନ୍ତି)
- **Do you take pride in your cultural and linguistic identity or do you try to hide behind the mainstream culture and language?** ଆପଣ ଆପଣଙ୍କ ଭାଷା ଓ ସଂସ୍କୃତି ପାଇଁ ଗର୍ବିତ କି? ନା ଆପଣ ପ୍ରଧାନଭାଷାର ଭାଷା ଓ ସଂସ୍କୃତି ସହିତ ମିଶିଯିବାକୁ ଚାହାନ୍ତି?
- **Is the language passed down from generation to generation? If not, why? What language is replacing it?** ବଂଶାନୁକ୍ରମେ ଆପଣ ଆପଣଙ୍କ ଭାଷାକୁ ବ୍ୟବହାର କରୁଛନ୍ତି କି? ଯଦି କରୁନାହାଁନ୍ତି ତେବେ କାହିଁକି କରୁନାହାଁନ୍ତି? ଆପଣଙ୍କ ଭାଷା ସ୍ଥାନରେ ଆପଣ ଅନ୍ୟ କେଉଁ ଭାଷା ବ୍ୟବହାର କରୁଛନ୍ତି?
- **Could you please indicate how often the members of each generation use the language**

with other generations (old people with old people, young people with old people, etc) in their informal contacts (in the street, at home, in leisure time...)? ଆପଣ କହିପାରିବେକି ଆପଣଙ୍କ ପରିବାରର ଲୋକେ ବଂଶ ପରଂପରାଂ କ୍ରମେ ଏହି ଭାଷାକୁ ବ୍ୟବହାର କରି ଆସୁଛନ୍ତି କି? (ବୟସ ବୃଦ୍ଧ ଲୋକେ ବୟସ ବୃଦ୍ଧ ଲୋକଙ୍କ ସହିତ କିମ୍ବା ପରିବାରର କମ୍ ବୟସର ଲୋକେ ବୃଦ୍ଧ ଲୋକଙ୍କ ସହିତ) ବଜାର ପରିସରରେ / ଘରେ / ଘରୋଇ ପରିବେଶରେ / ପରିବାର ବାହାରେ ସାଙ୍ଗସାଥୀ ମେଳରେ

The people...	*Elderly Men*	*Elderly Women*	*Adult Men*	*Adult Women*	*Young Men*	*Young Women*	*Boys*	*Girls*
Elderly Men								
Elderly Women								
Adult Men								
Adult Women								
Young Men								
Young Women								
Boys								
Girls								

Specify the frequency: 5 = always in this language; **4** = more in this language than others; **3** = equally often in either language; **2** = more in other languages than in this one; **1** = always in other languages.

ଯେଉଁମାନଙ୍କ ସହିତ ଆପଣ କଥା ହୁଅନ୍ତି . . .

ଲୋକମାନେ	ବରିଷ୍ଠ ଗୁରୁଜନ ପୁରୁଷ	ବରିଷ୍ଠ ଗୁରୁଜନ ମହିଳା	ବୟସ୍କ ପୁରୁଷ	ବୟସ୍କ ମହିଳା	ଯୁବକ	ଯୁବତୀ	ବାଳକ	ବାଳିକା
ବରିଷ୍ଠ ଗୁରୁଜନପୁରୁଷ								
ବରିଷ୍ଠ ଗୁରୁଜନ ମହିଳା								
ବୟସ୍କ ପୁରୁଷ								
ବୟସ୍କ ମହିଳା								
ଯୁବକ								
ଯୁବତୀ								
ବାଳକ								
ବାଳିକା								

କଥାବାର୍ତ୍ତା କରିବାର ପରିମାଣ :୫=ସର୍ବଦା ଏହି ଭାଷାରେ ୪=ଅନ୍ୟଭାଷା ଅପେକ୍ଷା ଏହି ଭାଷାରେ ଅଧିକାଂଶ ସମୟରେ ୩=ଏହି ଭାଷା / ଅନ୍ୟାନ୍ୟ ଭାଷାରେ ସମାନ ଭାବରେ ୨=ଏହି ଭାଷା ଅପେକ୍ଷା ଅନ୍ୟାନ୍ୟ ଭାଷାରେ ଅଧିକ ସମୟ ୧=ସର୍ବଦା ଅନ୍ୟାନ୍ୟ ଭାଷାରେ

- **Do the speakers of other languages speak this language? Under what circumstances?** ଅନ୍ୟାନ୍ୟ ଭାଷାର ଲୋକମାନେ ଏହି ଭାଷାରେ କଥା ହୁଅନ୍ତି କି? ଯଦି ହୁଅନ୍ତି ତେବେ କେଉଁ ଅବସ୍ଥାରେ?
- **Has any factor, political, economic or social, directly influenced the growth or threatened the future of the language?** ରାଜନୈତିକ, ଅର୍ଥନୈତିକ ବା ସାମାଜିକ ଭଳି କୌଣସି କାରଣ ଏହି ଭାଷାର ବିକାଶକୁ ବାଧାଦେଉଛି କିମ୍ବା ଏ ଭାଷାର ଭବିଷ୍ୟତ ପ୍ରତି ବିପଦ ସୃଷ୍ଟି କରୁଚି କି?
- **Is the language currently threatened? If so, what is the cause?** ବର୍ତ୍ତମାନ ସମୟରେ ଏ ଭାଷା ପ୍ରତି କିଛି ବିପଦ ଅଛି କି? କାରଣ କଣ?
- **What is the main economic activity of your community?** ଆପଣଙ୍କ ସମାଜ ବା ଜନଗୋଷ୍ଠିର ରୋଜଗାରର ପନ୍ଥା କ'ଣ?
- **Does the language have any official status (official, joint-official language, acceptance ...)?** ଏହି ଭାଷା ପାଇଁ ସରକାରୀ ସ୍ୱୀକୃତି ମିଳିଛି କି? କି ପ୍ରକାର ସ୍ୱୀକୃତି, ସରକାରୀ ସ୍ୱୀକୃତି / ସହଯୋଗୀ ସରକାରୀ ସ୍ୱୀକୃତି / ସରକାରୀ ସାହାଯ୍ୟ?
- **Is this language used in education (whether as the teaching medium or as a subject of study)? Indicate whether there is spoken and/or written use of the language in elementary education.** ଶିକ୍ଷାନୁଷ୍ଠାନ ବା ସ୍କୁଲ କଲେଜ ସ୍ତରରେ ଏହା ଶିକ୍ଷାର ମାଧ୍ୟମ ଭାବରେ ବା ଏକ ବିଷୟବସ୍ତୁ ଭାବରେ ଗ୍ରହଣ କରଯାଉଛି କି?
- **Is this language used in the media (radio, newspapers and television...)?** କୌଣସି ଗଣ-ମାଧମରେ ଏହି ଭାଷାକୁ ବ୍ୟବହାର କରାଯାଉଛି କି? ରେଡିଓ / ଖବରକାଗଜ / ଟେଲିଭିଜନ
- **Is this language used in religious services and ceremonies? Indicate whether there is spoken or written use of the language in religious services and ceremonies.** କୌଣସି ଧର୍ମୀୟ କାର୍ଯ୍ୟରେ ବା

ଧର୍ମୀୟ ଅନୁଷ୍ଠାନରେ ଏହି ଭାଷାର ବ୍ୟବହାର ଅଛି କି? ଏହି ସବୁ କ୍ଷେତ୍ରରେ ଏହା କଥିତ ଭାବରେ କିମ୍ବା ଲିଖିତ ଭାବରେ ବ୍ୟବହାର ହୋଇଥାଏ କି?

- **Is the language used in local business and commercial transactions?** ସ୍ଥାନୀୟ ବ୍ୟବସାୟୀମାନେ ବ୍ୟବସାୟ ବାଣିଜ୍ୟ କାରବାର କରିବା ସମୟରେ ଏହି ଭାଷା ବ୍ୟବହାର କରନ୍ତି କି?
- **Is there any government organisation or body responsible for linguistic policy and planning with respect to this language? What kind of activities does this organisation perform?** କୌଣସି ସରକାରୀ ସଂସ୍ଥା ବା ଅନୁଷ୍ଠାନ ଏହି ଭାଷା ବିକାଶ ପାଇଁ କୌଣସି ପଲିସି ବା ଯୋଜନା କାର୍ଯ୍ୟକାରୀ କରୁଛନ୍ତି କି? ଏଥିପାଇଁ ସେହି ଅନୁଷ୍ଠାନ କିଭଳି ପଦକ୍ଷେପ ସବୁ ଗ୍ରହଣ କରିଛନ୍ତି?
- **Are you aware of any kind of private cultural or linguistic organisation or body which promotes the awareness and/or use of the language? What kind of activities does this perform?** ଏହି ଭାଷାର ବିକାଶ ବା ଜନଗୋଷ୍ଠିଙ୍କ ସଂଖ୍ୟା ବୃଦ୍ଧି ପାଇଁ କୌଣସି ବେସରକାରୀ ସାଂସ୍କୃତିକ ବା ଭାଷା–ବିକାଶକାରୀ ସଂସ୍ଥା ବା ଅନୁଷ୍ଠାନ ସଚେତନତା ସୃଷ୍ଟି କରିବାକୁ ପଦକ୍ଷେପ ନେଉଛନ୍ତି କି?
- **Does the language have a literary tradition? If so, please give some information about this literary tradition.** ଏହି ଭାଷାର ସାହିତ୍ୟିକ ପରଂପରା ବିଷୟରେ ଆପଣ କିଛି ସୂଚନା ଦେଇପାରିବେ କି?
- **In your view, what is the attitude of the general public towards the knowledge and use of this language?** ଏହି ଭାଷା ବ୍ୟବହାର କରୁଥିବା ଲୋକମାନଙ୍କର ଭାଷା ବ୍ୟବହାର ବିଷୟରେ ବା ଭାଷା ବିଷୟରେ କିଭଳି ଧାରଣ ରହିଛି?
- **Are you concerned about the preservation of your language or you believe it hardly matters as long as you are able to communicate in some language or the other?** ଏହି ଭାଷାର ସୁରକ୍ଷା ପାଇଁ ଆପଣ ଚିନ୍ତିତ କି? ନା ଯେକୌଣସି ଭାଷାରେ ବି ଆପଣ କଥାବାର୍ତ୍ତା କରିପାରିଲେ ତାହା ଆପଣଙ୍କ ପାଇଁ ଯଥେଷ୍ଟ କି?

- **If your answer is yes to above, could you please give some suggestions as to what could be done by the government or the people themselves, for the long-term sustenance of such minority languages.** ଯଦି ଉପରୋକ୍ତ ପ୍ରଶ୍ନର ଉତ୍ତର ହଁ ତେବେ ଏହି ସବୁ ଭାଷାର କେଉଁଭଳି ସୁରକ୍ଷା ଲୋକମାନଙ୍କଦ୍ୱାରା ବା ସରକାରଙ୍କ ଦ୍ୱାରା ହୋଇପାରିବ ତାହା ଉପରେ କିଛି ତଥ୍ୟ ପ୍ରଦାନ ଦୟାକରି ପ୍ରଦାନ କରନ୍ତୁ ।

PLEASE ADD ANY OTHER DETAILS REGARDING THE SITUATION OF YOUR LANGUAGE WHICH YOU CONSIDER TO BE OF INTEREST. At the same time, we would be grateful if you could give us any information, statistics or reports that might help us better understand the situation of this language. It would also be very helpful if you could provide the addresses of any individuals or bodies that may be able to offer further data about this language. ଏହି ଭାଷା ବିଷୟରେ ଆପଣ କୌଣସି ମୂଲ୍ୟବାନ ସୂଚନା ଦେବାକୁ ଚାହିଁବେ କି? ଏହି ଭାଷା ବିଷୟରେ କିଛି ରିପୋର୍ଟ, ତଥ୍ୟ, ଗବେଷଣା ସଂବନ୍ଧୀୟ ସୂଚନା ପ୍ରଭୃତି ଆପଣ ଆମକୁ ପ୍ରଦାନ କରିବାକୁ ଚାହିଁବେ କି? ଏଥିପାଇଁ କୌଣସି ବ୍ୟକ୍ତି ବିଶେଷ ବା ଅନ୍ୟାନ୍ୟ ସୂତ୍ରର ଠିକଣା ବା ସୂଚନା କେନ୍ଦ୍ର ବିଷୟରେ ଆମକୁ ସୂଚନା ପ୍ରଦାନ କରନ୍ତୁ ।

Thank you very much for your kind cooperation.

Bibliography

Abbi, Anvita (ed.) (1997). *Languages of Tribal and Indigenous Peoples of India: The Ethnic Space.* New Delhi: Motilal Banarasidass.

Abdel Rahim Hamid Mugaddam. (2005). "Language Attitudes and Language Shift among Ethnic Migrants in Khartoum." Retrieved 10 May 2011 from www.afrikanistik-online.de/archiv/2005/181/ -

Adegbija, E. (1992). "Survival Strategies for Minority Languages: A Case-study of Oko." *International Journal of the Sociology of Language. 102*: 153-73.

Aitchison, J. (1981). *Language Change: Progress or Decay.* London: Fontana Paperbacks.

Akere, Funso. (1981) *Sociolinguistic Consequences of Language Contact: English verses Nigerian Languages.* Language Sciences, Vol. 3, Issue 2.

Annamalai, E. (1997). "Questions on the Linguistic Characteristics of the Tribal Languages of India" (pp. 15-23), in A. Abbi (ed.). *Languages of Tribal and Indigenous Peoples of India*, Delhi: Motilal Banarsidass Publishers.

Annamalai, E. (2001) *Managing Multilingualism in India: Political and Linguistic Manifestations*. New Delhi: Sage.

Annamalai, E. (ed.). *Language Movements in India.* CIIL Conferences and Seminar Series – 5.

Annual Report (2009-10). Ministry of Tribal Affairs. Government of India.

Berry, J.W. (1990). "Psychology of Acculturation", In J. Berman (Ed.), *Cross-cultural Perspectives: Nebraska Symposium on Motivation, Vol.* 37 (pp. 201-234). Lincoln, NE: University of Nebraska Press.

Berry, J.W. (2003). "Multicultural Attitudes and Identities in Canada." In J.W. Berry, R.C. Mishra and R.C. Tripathi (Eds.), *Psychology in Human and Social Development* (pp. 138-154). New Delhi: Sage.

Berry, J.W. and Sam, D.L. (1997). "Acculturation and Adaptation". In J.W. Berry; M.S. Segall, and C. Kagitcibasi (Eds.), *Handbook of Cross-cultural Psychology: Vol. 3, Social Behavior and Applications (2nd ed.,* pp. 291-326). Needham Heights, MA: Allyn and Bacon.

Bhatia, T.K. and Ritchie, W.C. (2004) "Bilingualism in the Global Media and Advertising". In T.K. Bhatia and W.C. Ritchie (Eds.), *The Handbook of Bilingualism* (pp. 513-546). Blackwell Publishing Ltd.

Bloomfield, L. (1933) *Language and Linguistics.* New York: Henry Holt.

Bose, Nirmal Kumar. (1977). *Tribal Life in India, New Delhi:* National Book Trust.

Cerný, M. (2010). "Language Death versus Language Survival: A Global Perspective." In *Beyond Globalisation: Exploring the Limits of Globalisation in the Regional Context* (conference proceedings), 51-56. Ostrava: University of Ostrava Czech Republic. http://conference.osu.eu/globalization/publ/06-cerny.pdf.

Chatterjee, S.K. (1973). *India - A Polyglot Nation and its Linguistic Problems*, Bombay, M.G. Memorial Research Centre, Hindustan Prachar Sabha.

Coyle, Martin, Peter Garside, Malcolm Kelsall and John Peck (edt.) (1990). *Encyclopaedia of Literature and Criticism*. London: Routledge. pp. 976-990.

Cummins, Jim (2009). "Fundamental Psychological and Sociological Principles underlying Educational Success for Linguistic Minority Students." In Mohanty, Ajit, Minati Panda, Robert Phillipson and Tove Skutnabb-Kangas (eds), *Multilingual Education for Social Justice: Globalising the Local*. New Delhi: Orient Blackswan, 21-35.

Crystal, David. (2000) *Language Death.* Cambridge: Cambridge University Press.

Dan, Ben-Amos. (1982). *Folklore in Context. Essays.* New Delhi, Madras: South Asian Publishers.

Das, Kunja Behari and L.K. Mahapatra. (1993). *Folklore of Odisha*, New Delhi: National Book Trust.

Dash, J. (1996). "Tribal Heritage in Culture and Society." In P.K. Mishra (ed), *Comprehensive History and Culture of Orissa, Volume: 2.* New Delhi: Kaveri Books.

Del Pilar, J.A. and Udasco, J.O. (2004). Deculturation: Its lack of validity. *Cultural Diversity and Ethnic Minority Psychology, 10*, 169-176.

Devy, G.N. (2002). *Painted Words: An Anthology of Tribal Literature*. New Delhi: Penguin Books.

Dhal, G. B. (1976). *Bhasashastra Parichaya.* Bhubaneswar: Odisha State Bureau of Textbook Preparation and Production.

Dorais, L.J. (1995). Language, culture and identity: Some Inuit examples. *The Canadian Journal of Native Studies, 15,* 293–306. Retrieved on May 12, 2010, from http://www.brandonu.ca/Library/CJNS/15.2/dorais.pdf

Elias, V. (2008). The Implications of Modernity for Language Retention and Related Identity Issues: Applying the Thought of Charles Taylor. International Congress on Arctic Social Sciences (ICASS VI), hosted by the International Arctic Social Sciences Association (IASSA), Nuuk, Greenland, August 22–26, 2008.

Ellis, R. (1991). *Understanding Second Language Acquisition*. Oxford: OUP.

Elwin, Verrier. (1943). *The Aborginals.* New Delhi: Oxford University Press.

Elwin, Verrier. (1954). *Tribal Myths of Odisha.* Bombay: Oxford University Press.

Fasold, R. (1987). *The Sociolinguistics of Society.* Oxford: Basil Blackwell.

Fishman, J. A. (1996). "What Do You Lose When You Lose Your Language?" In G. Cantoni (Ed.), *Stabilising Indigenous Ianguages.* Flagstaff: Center for Excellence in Education, Northern Arizona University. Retrieved June 11, 2010, from http://www.ncela.gwu.edu/pubs/stabilize/iiifamilies/lose.htm

Foster, G.M. (1953). "What is Folk Culture?" *American Anthropologist*, Vol-IV (I), p-159.

Gardner, R.C. and W.E. Lambert (1972). *Attitudes and Motivations in Second Language Learning.* Rowley Mass: New Bury House Publishers.

Ghosh, Jayati. "The Loss of Language." *Frontline.* Volume 23 - Issue 2, Jan. 28 - Feb. 10, 2006.

Grierson, G.A. (Reprinted 1968). *Linguistic Survey of India. Volume V: Indo-Aryan Family (Eastern group), Part– II: Bihari and Odia Languages.* Govt. of India, Delhi: Motilal Banarassidas.

Hasnain, S. I. (1997). "New Economic Policy and the Fate of Minority Languages." In S. Ramakrishna (ed.) *Translation and Multilingualism: Postcolonial Context.* Delhi: Pencraft International.

Heugh, Kathleen (2009). Literacy and Bi/multilingual Education in Africa: Recovering Collective Memory and Knowledge. In Mohanty, Ajit, Minati Panda, Robert Phillipson and Tove Skutnabb-Kangas (eds). *Multilingual Education for Social Justice: Globalising the Local.* New Delhi: Orient Blackswan, 95-113.

Hough, David, Ram Bahadur Thapa Magar and Amrit Yonjan-Tamang (2009). 'Privileging Indigenous Knowledges: Empowering MLE in Nepal.' In Mohanty,

Ajit, Minati Panda, Robert Phillipson and Tove Skutnabb-Kangas (eds). *Multilingual Education for Social Justice: Globalising the Local*. New Delhi: Orient Longman, 146-161.

Ishtiaq, M. (1997). "Typology of Language Change and Maintenance among the Santals and Mundas" (pp. 335-359), in A. Abbi (ed.), *Languages of Tribal and Indigenous Peoples of India*, Delhi: Motilal Banarsidass Publishers.

Ishtiaq, M. (1999). *Language Shifts among the Scheduled Tribes in India.* New Delhi: MLBD.

Kaul, Omkar, D.P. Pattanayak and P. Umarani. (2001). *Sociolinguistics and Language Education: A Festschrift for Dr. D.P. Pattanayak.* New Delhi: Creative Books.

Kerketta, D (2004). *Oraon Bhāsā Sikhyana Pustikā.* Academy of Tribal Dialects and Culture, Government of Odisha.

Khubchandani, L.M. (1997). *Revisualising Boundaries and Plurilingual Ethos.* New Delhi: Sage Publications.

Krauss, Michael. (1992). "The World's Languages in Crisis." *Language 68(1).*1-42.

Kujur, M. (2006). *Sadri Bhāsā Sikhyana Pustikā.* Academy of Tribal Dialects and Culture, Government of Odisha.

Kundu, M. (1990). "Tribal Education in India – Some Problems" (pp. 246-254), in: B. Chaudhuri (ed.), *Education and Literacy Programmes*. Delhi: Mittal Publications.

Kundu, M. (1994). *Tribal Education: New Perspectives*. New Delhi: Gyan Publishing House.

Lambert, Wallace E. (1977). "The Effects of Bilingualism on the Individual: Cognitive and Sociocultural Consequences." *Bilingualism: Psychological, Social, and Educational Implications,* edited by Peter A. Hornby. New York: Academic Press.

Language Vitality and Endangerment. UNESCO Ad Hoc

Expert Group on Endangered Languages. Document submitted to the *International Expert Meeting on UNESCO Programme Safeguarding of Endangered Languages,* Paris, 10–12 March 2003.

Macnamara, J. (1969). "How Can One Measure the Extent of a Person's Bilingual Capacity? In L.G. Kelly (Ed.), *Description and Measurement of Bilingualism* (pp. 80-97). Toronto: University of Toronto Press.

Mahapatra, L.K. and Dash, J. (1996). "Tribal Cultures of Orissa." In P.K. Mishra (ed), *Comprehensive History and Culture of Orissa, Volume: 2.* New Delhi: Kaveri Books.

Mahapatra, B.P. (1979). "Santali Language Movement in the Context of Many Dominant Languages". *International Journal of the Sociology of Language* 75: 73-78.

Mahapatra, K. (1997). "Tribal Languages of Odisha." In *Tribal Languages and Culture of Odisha,* (Ed.) K. Mahapatra. Bhubaneswar: Academy of Tribal Dialects and Culture, Government of Odisha.

Mahapatra, K. (1998). Linguistic Landscape and Literary Cultivation. *Adivasi.* Vol. XXXVIII, Nos. 1 and 2.

Mahapatra, Sitakanta. (1997). "The Celebration of Life." *Tribal Language and Culture of Odisha.* (Ed.) K. Mahapatra. Bhubaneswar: Academy of Tribal Dialects and Culture, Government of Odisha.

Majumdar, D.N. (1944). *Races and Cultures of lndia,* Delhi: Asia Publishing House.

Malekar, Anosh. *InfoChange News and Features,* April 2010. Retrieved April 27 2011 from infochangeindia.org/.../The-loss-of-languages-What's-all-the-fuss-about.html

Masica, Colin P. (1993). *The Indo-Aryan Languages.* Cambridge: Cambridge University Press.

Mishra, M.K. (1992). *Paschima Odisara Adibasi Lok Sahitya.* Bhubaneswar: Academy of Tribal Dialects and Culture, Govt. of India.

Mishra, M.K. (1997). "Ethnic Identity and Oral Narratives: A Case Study on Kamars of Odisha." *Tribal Language and Culture of Odisha*. (Ed.) K. Mahapatra. Bhubaneswar: Academy of Tribal Dialects and Culture, Government of Odisha.

Mohanty, A.K. (1994). *Bilingualism in a Multilingual Society*. Mysore: Central Institute of Indian Languages.

Mohanty, Ajit K. (1995). *Bilingualism in a Multilingual Society. Psycho-social and Pedagogical Implications*. Mysore: Central Institute of Indian Languages.

Mohanty, A.K. and Parida, S. (1993). *Bilingualism and Attitude towards Language and cultural Maintenance and Integration in a Tribal-non-tribal Contact Situation*. Unpublished manuscript, CAS in Psychology, Utkal University, Bhubaneswar, India.

Mohanty, Ajit. K and Saikia, J. *Bilingualism and Intergroup Relationship in Tribal and Non-Tribal Contact Situations* Retrieved: ebooks.iaccp.org/xian/PDFs/4_2Mohanty.pdf

Mohanty, Ajit K. (2000). "Perpetuating Inequality: The Disadvantage of Language, Minority Mother Tongues and Related Issues." In Mohanty, Ajit K. and Misra, Girishwar (eds). *Psychology of Poverty and Disadvantage*. New Delhi: Concept Publishing Company, 104-117.

Mohanty, Ajit K. (2006). "Multilingualism of the Unequals and Predicaments of Education in India: Mother Tongue or Other Tongue?" In García, Ofelia, Skutnabb-Kangas, Tove and Torres-Guzmán, María (eds). *Imagining Multilingual Schools. Languages in Education and Glocalisation*. Clevedon, Buffalo and Toronto: Multilingual Matters, 262-283.

Mohanty, Ajit K. (2007). Introduction. In Skutnabb-Kangas, Tove, *Bilingualism or not – the Education of minorities*. New Delhi: Orient Blackswan.

Mohanty, Ajit K. (2009). "Multilingual Education – A Bridge Too Far?" In Mohanty, Ajit, Minati Panda, Robert Phillipson and Tove Skutnabb-Kangas (eds). *Multilingual*

Education for Social Justice: Globalising the Local. New Delhi: Orient Blackswan.

The National Policy of Education. 1986.

Nettle, D and S. Romaine. (2001). *Vanishing Voices*. Oxford: Oxford University Press.

Ota, A.B., F. Bara and K. Patnaik (ed.) (2010). *Dimensions of Tribal Education in Odisha*. Schedule Castes and Scheduled Tribes Research and Training Institute, Bhubaneswar.

Panda, Minati and Ajit Mohanty (2009). 'MLE Plus: Culture to Classroom'. In Mohanty, Ajit, Minati Panda, Robert Phillipson and Tove Skutnabb-Kangas (eds). *Multilingual Education for Social Justice: Globalising the Local*. New Delhi: Orient Blackswan, 295-312.

Pandharipande, R.V. (2002). "Minority Matters: Issues in Minority Languages in India." *International Journal on Multicultural Societies*. Vol. 4, No. 2. <http://www.unesco.org/most/vl4n2pandhari.pdf>.

Pasayat, C. (2003). *Glimpses of Tribal and Folk Culture*. New Delhi: Anmol Publications Pvt. Ltd.

Patel, P. (1995). *Sadri,* Academy of Tribal Dialects and Culture, Government of Odisha.

Patel, P.N. (1997). "Demographic profile of tribal Odisha." In *Tribal Languages and Culture of Odisha,* Academy of Tribal Dialects and Culture, Government of Odisha.

Pati, R.N. and Dash, J. (2002). *Tribal and Indigenous People of India: Problems and Prospects.* New Delhi: APH Publishers.

Pati, Biswamoy. (2011). "Introduction." In B.Pati (ed), *Adivasis in Colonial India: Survival, Resistance and Negotiation.* New Delhi: Orient Blackswan.

Patnaik, N. (2002). *Folklore of Tribal Communities.* New Delhi: Gyan Publishing House.

Patnaik, N. (1988). "The impact of Industrial and Mining Activities in Tribal Areas". *Adivasi*, Vol. XXVIII, No. 3, 4. December, 1988.

Pattanayak, D.P. (1981). *Multilingualism and Mother Tongue Education*. Delhi: Oxford University Press.

Pattanayak, D.P. (1990). *Multilingualism in India*. UK: Multilingual Matters Ltd.

Pattanayak, D.P. *Language Education and Culture*. CIIL Occasional Monograph Series – 46, CIIL, Mysore.

Pattanayak, D.P. (ed) *Language Law and National Integration*. CIIL Occasional Monograph Series – 36, CIIL, Mysore.

Prasad, N.K. (1979). *The Language Issue in India*. Delhi: Leeladevi Publications.

Raza, Moonis and Aijazuddin Ahmad (eds.). (1990). *An Atlas of Tribal India*. New Delhi: Concept Publishing Company.

Rhydwen, M. (1998). "Strategies for Doing the Impossible." In Oslter (ed.), 101-106.

Richards, J., J. Platt and H. Webber (1985). *Longman Dictionary of Applied Linguistics*. Harlow: Longman.

Rogers, Carl. (1959). "A Theory of Therapy, Personality and Interpersonal Relationships as Developed in the Client-centered Framework. In (ed.) S. Koch, *Psychology: A Study of a Science. Vol. 3: Formulations of the Person and the Social Context*. New York: McGraw Hill.

Romaine, Suzanne. (1995). *Bilingualism* (2nd ed.). Oxford: Blackwell Publishers.

Roy Burman, B.K. (1969). "Languages of Tribal Communities in India and their Use in Primary Education". In: N. Roy, ed., *Language and Society in India*, 251–69. Simla: Indian Institute of Advanced Study.

"Save Dying Languages to Preserve Rich Heritage." (2012, July 8), *The New Indian Express,* New Delhi.

Sen, Amartya (1985). *Commodities and Capabilities*. Amsterdam: North Holland.

Singh, K.S. and Manoharan, S. (1993). *Languages and Scripts.* Delhi: Oxford University Press

Singh K.S., S. Manoharan and R. Thirumalai. (1997). *People of India*. New Delhi: East-West Press.

Singh, T.R. (1966). "Some aspects of ritual purity and pollution," *The Eastern Anthropologist*, Vol. 19, No. 2.

Skutnabb-Kangas, Tove (2000). *Linguistic Genocide in Education - or Worldwide Diversity and Human Rights?* Mahwah, NJ and London, UK: Lawrence Erlbaum Associates. South Asian updated edition in 2008, Delhi: Orient BlackSwan.

Skutnabb-Kangas, Tove (2008). "Human Rights and Language Policy in Education." In Volume 1. *Language Policy and Political Issues in Education*, eds. Stephen May and Nancy H. Hornberger. *Encyclopedia of Language and Education*, 2nd edition. New York: Springer, 107-119.

Skutnabb-Kangas, Tove (2009). "MLE for Global Justice: Issues, Approaches, Opportunities". In Skutnabb-Kangas, Tove, Phillipson, Robert, Mohanty, Ajit and Panda, Minati (eds). *Social Justice through Multilingual Education*. Bristol: Multilingual Matters.

Skutnabb-Kangas, Tove. (2009). *India, Tribal Education, and Participating in Crimes against Humanity*. Short article in *NFCS Newsletter (National Folklore Support Center, Chennai, www.indianfolklore.org)*.

Sridhar, K.K. (1996). "Societal Multilingualism". In S.L. McKay and N.H. Hornberger (eds.) *Sociolinguistics and Language Teaching*. Cambridge: Cambridge University Press.

Srivastava, R. (1984). "Linguistic Minorities and National Language". In Florian Coulmas, (ed.), *Linguistic Minorities and Literacy: Language Policy Issues in Developing Countries*, 99–114. Berlin: Mouton de Gruyter.

"The Precipitious Decline of Languages is Worrying." (2013, March 2). *The New Indian Express*, New Delhi.

Thomason, A. (1999). "Tribal Identity and Loss of Self." *Indigenous People.*

Tribes of Odisha (2004). Schedule Castes and Scheduled Tribes Research and Training Institute, Bhubaneswar.

Tribal Welfare Department. (1994). *Tribal Education in Odisha in the Context of Education for all by 2000 A.D.: A Status Paper*. Bhubaneswar: Tribal Welfare Department, Government of Odisha.

Tyagi, R.S. and P.C. Mahapatra. (2000). *Educational Administration in Odisha. Structures, Processes and Future Prospects.* New Delhi: Vikas Publishing House.

Ulrich, Ammon, Norbert Dittmar and Klaus J. Mattheier. (2006). *Sociolinguistics: an International Handbook of the Science of Language and Society*, Volume 3. Berlin: Walter de Gruyter,

Vidyarthi, Lalita Prasad. (1979). *Rise of Anthropology in India: a Social Science Orientation, Volume 1.* New Delhi: Concept Publishing Company.

Wardhaugh, Ronald. (2009). *An Introduction to Sociolinguistics*. United Kingdom: John Wiley and Sons Ltd.

Wurm, Stephen A. (ed.) (2001). *Atlas of the World's Languages in Danger of Disappearing.* Second edition. Paris: UNESCO Publishing.

Xaxa, V. (2005). "Politics of Language, Religion and Identity: Tribes in India". *Economic and Political Weekly,* Vol. 40, No. 13, pp. 63-70.

Zide, N.H. (1997). "Changing Tribal Languages". In *Tribal Languages and Culture of Odisha,* Academy of Tribal Dialects and Culture, Government of Odisha.

Zide, Norman. (2001) "Santali." In Jane Garry and Carl Rubino (eds.). *Facts About the World's Languages: An Encyclopaedia of the World's Major Languages: Past and Present*. New York / Dublin: H. W. Wilson Press.

Illustrations

A Tribal Couple of Sundargarh.

Tribal Ladies.

A Tribal Lady Selling the Local Brew Handia.

A Community Meeting.

A Tribal Lady Selling her Wares.

A Tribal Lady Collecting Firewood.

Data Collection in Progress at Bargaon Girls High School, Bhoipali, Sundargarh District.

The Two Research Assistants at Bhoipali.

Karma Festival in Progress at Orampada, Rourkela.

Tribal Festivities in Progress.

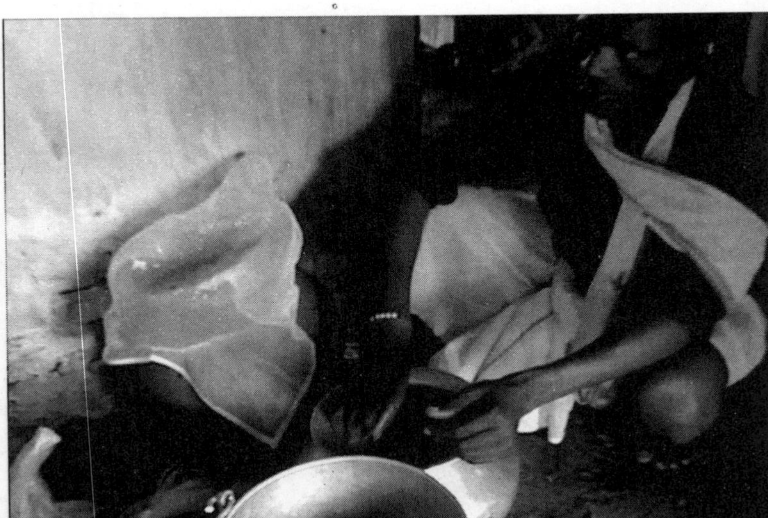

Handia Preparation.

Index

T